Reality Of A Fantasy Called Love

OrangeBooks Publication

Smriti Nagar, Bhilai, Chhattisgarh - 490020

Website: **www.orangebooks.in**

First Edition, 2022

ISBN: 978-93-5621-012-7

REALITY OF A FANTASY CALLED LOVE

RUDRA DAVE

OrangeBooks Publication

www.orangebooks.in

ACKNOWLEDGEMENT

I would like to acknowledge and extend my heartfelt gratitude to my parents for their constant support in encouraging me to follow my passion for writing. I would also like to acknowledge the perspectives and opinions of hundreds of strangers that I have observed and interacted with on social media, at railway platforms, airports, waiting areas, various events, in trains, buses, flights and many other places which enabled me to think holistically about relationships and understand human nature. I would like to thank god and the universe for their blessings and positive energies that made everything possible. Finally, the most important of all — thank you to my readers for picking up this book. I had a great time writing this one.

Happy reading!

Index

Chapter 1
"The Reality Of Love" 1

Chapter 2
"The Negative List" 22

Chapter 3
"Recipe For A Long Lasting Relationship" 44

Chapter 4
"Shattering Myths" 63

Chapter 5
"Common Conflicts" 86

Chapter 6
"Infidelity" 100

Chapter 7
"Heartbreak" 111

Chapter 8
"Love Hacks" 121

Chapter 9
"Letters Of Wisdom" 141

Chapter 10
"Important Trending Topics" 167

CHAPTER 1

"THE REALITY OF LOVE"

Love is overrated! Oh, you didn't expect this line from a *"Self-help book"* on love and relationships, right? Well, I am just getting started. Before you judge me, let me tell you that I am no skeptic or a heartbroken pessimist. Then why did I use that first line? Just to have a sensational opening line for my first book? Nope. I said it because I am a realist. I am very much aware of the reality and unfortunately, love or the *"idea of being in love"* in our minds is far from reality and is just a mere conjectured fantasy.

Have you ever completely fallen for someone, only to later realize that person wasn't at all who you thought they were?

Have you ever obsessed about the future with someone that you don't actually know very well?

Have you ever been completely blind-sided by someone's actions not matching their words?

If you answered yes to any of the above, you might have a habit of falling in love with *"fantasies"*.

If you have unreasonably unrealistic ideas about love that you have formed by watching Romantic Comedies or by reading delusory fairytale love stories, then reading this book will be an eye opening experience for you.

So let's get started. Brace yourself for this *"reality ride"* where we shall discuss many unsaid truths (unapologetically and unabashedly) about love, relationships, breakups, emotions and much more, which will widen your horizon and make you more aware.

Instead of asking you to behave in a *"standard manner"* as defined by the society and its countless stereotypes, I want you to be self-reliant and discover who you are and create your own path. So, let's drink from the same cup of life yet remain our true selves — two souls joined yet forever unique.

In present times, we see a lot of relationships crumbling down. The COVID-19 pandemic has shown a sharp rise in break-ups and divorces. Disrupted routines and the removal of external leisure activities left many couples struggling, according to the experts.

There has been 35% spike in divorce cases all over the world due to the lockdowns. Marriage counseling has found an increase of almost 20% in family and couple counseling sessions compared to the sessions before the lockdown. Being in a relationship is not an easy task these days. Love has become text messages and phone calls. Love has become Instagram posts, Snapchat and staring at a screen.

Love has become more about hook ups and swiping right and left on dating apps instead of having an emotional depth and commitment in a relationship. Love these days has become crawling back to a person who has hurt, manipulated and lied to you. People are so empty and lonely that they mistake mere attention for love and eventually get their heart broken. People have convinced themselves that brokenness and devastation is what "tough love" looks like and it will get better with time. Many people are scared to fall in love. Why? What are the issues? How to prevent or overcome those problems? How to have a long lasting relationship? These are some of the questions which this book will answer and help its readers to figure out more about their relationship, their partner and themselves.

In the times we live in, love and heartbreak have become interchangeable words. The patience and tolerance level of almost everyone has reduced drastically. The smallest of things result into breakups and divorces. Does this mean there is no love left between couples?

The answer is a big NO.

Shocked?

Well, we are just getting started.

If you have ever loved someone, it can never die down. Love is a one-way thing. It is born inside us, we nurture it and it is ours. It can never expire. Just like after reading a book we cannot un-read it or after watching a movie we cannot un-watch it, similarly we cannot un-love people. The intensity of it may vary, but still love remains alive within us.

We can never be completely indifferent to someone we have ever loved, even if we are not on talking terms with that person anymore.

"Love has no death."

Yes, we learn to move on. That is what most people do after they get separated. They simply move on. But the love inside them still exists. They are simply oblivious to its existence inside them. Then they find someone else and a new love is born inside them. This does not mean that the new love overrides the previous love(s). They simply co-exist, just the priority levels change. So, if you have ever loved someone, broken up, moved on and you think that the love does not exist inside you anymore for that person, then WAKE UP! You are fooling yourself.

Perhaps you don't feel it as strongly as you once used to, but it exists. We can hate them or not respect them anymore but cannot un-love them. You may never even want to see their face again but you can never really kill the love you have for them, inside you.

For example, if there is a scale of 0-100 to measure your love for someone after your separation, then the least can be 1, it can never be 0. Probably that is one of the reasons that many end up patching up with their ex-lovers easily, be friends with them or some people may even hook up with them whenever they get a chance.

It is quite risky though. As they say, never let an old flame burn you twice. It can also be dangerous if you have moved on to a new partner and you also have constant interactions with your ex-lover.

The feeling of love that had become 1 post breakup can increase when you indulge in constant communication with your ex. It can ruin your current relationship if you are unable to control your subdued love for your ex (which might surpass your love for your current partner).

My personal advice — have a respectful distance with your ex if you ever loved them at any given point of time (birthday wishes or occasional small talk permissible) or completely avoid any sort of association if you cannot control your emotions. This will help you to sustain your current relationship with your partner. However, if you have genuinely met someone with whom you connect at a soul level and they completely understand you, and you both have a history together, but you feel it's not worth to lose that person just because a mere romance didn't work, then you can surely have them in your life, but better to set boundaries that don't hinder your current relationship as well as theirs.

So friends, don't lie to yourself and believe that you have absolutely no feeling left for someone you once loved. This may be a bitter pill to swallow but the truth is that it is not possible to un-love. You don't agree? Wanna debate? If you think you have un-loved your ex then there can be two conclusions. First one is that you never really loved them. The second conclusion is that you are deluded. If you still don't agree with me, then do one experiment (at your own risk) — just get back in touch with your ex-lover and have a platonic relationship.

Interact with them daily and do all those things which you do with a *"normal friend"* like share your feelings and thoughts over phone calls and meetings, gossip about people, go for movies, road-trips, dinners and holidays, celebrate festivals and birthdays. You will soon realize that your feelings (which you thought had gone) are coming back. Actually they never went away, they were just suppressed. Now with regular interactions those feelings have started flowing beyond your own control. The fact is that you simply cannot be *"normal friends"* with your former lover. You can be friends with boundaries, clarity and understanding but can never be like *"any other friend"*, a constant effort to keep things under control will always be required. In simple words, love can blossom again. It may be good for you, it may not be. But it can be grown back (we like it or not). And having a small seed of love inside us for anyone is not a bad thing. It is completely normal. We all have a lot of space inside us to sustain love for every person who has been a part of our life. The only wrong approach of dealing with it is that most people carry it as a burden and an emotional baggage. They go through a dilemma and have constant battles inside them.

They try to convince themselves that the people they loved were not appropriate (and probably they were not, some were obnoxious too), but the best thing is to simply accept that we have love for them inside us — for the time we spent and for the person we were when we were together, live with those happy memories and be at peace. Some people can be in our hearts but not in our lives. Accept that and move on.

But have you ever wondered that if love still exists inside us then why are people so intolerant towards each other that they get separated?

Is love not enough to sustain a relationship?

What else is required other than love to have a happy long lasting relationship?

Well, there are many answers to such questions, which we shall discover in the later chapters.

So, for time being forget about heartbreaks and separation. Let's start on a happy note and talk about the thing which we all crave for in our lives, which is LOVE (we may or may not admit it openly). Some of you are in love; others may be looking for love. Some of you will say *"I do not have time for this shit. I have different priorities"* but then you may secretly, deep inside want to experience love (may be you are yourself not aware of what you want or to be precise, what you need).

"We all need love and all we need is love."

So, what exactly is love?

Love cannot be defined. If someone could have defined love, they would have by now. It is intangible. Abstract. Cannot be touched or seen, just felt. You want to experience the feeling of love? Just close your eyes and think about the person you are romantically attracted to. Feels good right? Repeat it but this time think of your parents, friends or relatives that you genuinely care about. You must have felt two different feelings.

The first one can cause a bit of stir inside you, heartbeats get fast causing intense adrenaline rush of excitement and stimulation with a bit of anxiousness and nervousness. The latter one is calmer and more peaceful. So, these are just two variants of love which we talked about but there are many types of love that we generate like love for food, love for animals, love for sports, love for shopping etc.

We cannot compare them with each other. Ever read a meme on social media which said *"Love Pizza, it will never break your heart"*? Well, Pizza will satisfy your hunger but not your romantic desires and fantasies.

Love is incomparable, *for example* - love for one person cannot be compared with love for another person since the relationship, the journey, the timing, the internal and external conflicts and the emotions exists in totally different circumstances.

Similarly, love for a thing (like bag, phone, watch etc.) cannot be compared with love for other things or other human beings. Imagine how bizarre it would sound if you say *"I love you"* to someone and in the next sentence tell them *"I love your shoes!"* So the person you are romantically attracted to and for whom you closed your eyes, ever wondered why you love them? Is it even love? Or is it just an infatuation or admiration of certain qualities which they possess?

Some people say love cannot be described in words, it can only be felt. I agree.

It cannot be described, only be felt...but that feeling is not exclusive to just one person. It may happen that you may feel the same thing about another person or probably few people.

It means that you admire, respect, get attracted to so many people in your life, then how can you pick one and say it is love? How to differentiate between love and a mere infatuation?

Love is subjective and has different definitions for different people. To understand what love is, it is more important to know what is NOT love.

We think love is sharing details about our day, physical intimacy, posting pictures with each other on social media with romantic captions, mutually expressing our liking for each other, constantly texting or calling each other, going out for movies, dinners, holidays, parties, having exclusive priority over others, living together etc. The above mentioned activities are some of the things which we normally do with the people we like. But does that mean it is love? Certainly not.

Confused?

Calm down fellas. Let me explain...but before talking about love, I want to express my irritation towards a much abused term these days - *"True Love"*.

There is no such thing as true love. What does it even mean? Does it mean there is something called *"False Love"* as well? Love is simply love.

It does not require any adjective to show how real it is. It itself is the highest form of feeling which one can have for someone or something.

The word *"True"* before *"Love"* itself degrades the word *"Love"*.

For example, if one guy says *"I love you"* and another guy says *"I truly love you"*, in almost all cases the latter guy would be preferred over the first guy. But in reality both are saying exactly the same thing. Love is love only when it is true and comes from within. Saying *"I love you"* or *"I love this thing or place"* is enough to express your feeling.

The problem today is that there is not much understanding of *"Love"* among people. Using any adjective before *"Love"* in a way reduces the value of simply using the word *"Love"*.

So, the next time you hear someone talk about *"True Love"*, ask them what does it mean and what the difference is between love and true love. Most of them will not have an answer.

So then what is love? I have a personal list of observations which I like to call the "*Love Tests*".

You can use them and become aware of what love is and what is not.

So what is *the first test of love*?

It is very simple. When someone is more important to you than your own self.

Lord Buddha (as per Google) has explained the difference between like and love perfectly. He said, "When you like a flower, you just pluck it. But when you love a flower, you water it daily. One who understands this, understands life." Love is when you think of someone before yourself. Some people say your own happiness is the most important thing and I agree, but when you are in love, you get happy when they are happy.

"Their happiness is a source of your happiness."

Their happiness and well-being is the top priority and prevails over everything else. Putting someone ahead of you is a sign of love. Most *"practical people"* or the *"pseudo-intellectuals"* may call it stupidity. And perhaps if the relationship doesn't work out, even you might think that you were being so stupid and wasted so much of your time, missed so many opportunities blah blah blah. And that is a completely valid observation. But the catch here is, that if your partner is also in love with you, then they will also put you ahead of themselves. And this is where most love stories are successful. Both of them lookout for each other. They have each other's back.

"You take care of me and I will take care of you."

There is an unshakeable trust that is generated as a result of prioritizing each other consistently. The *second litmus test* of love is when there are no conditions involved. You must have heard a term highly used these days — *"Unconditional Love"*. People, who often use this term, don't understand the actual meaning of this phrase.

They simply say, *"It means there should not be any conditions in love."* Duh! Sounds too preachy, idealistic and unrealistic, right? But let's get deeper into this.

I think there should be conditions, but not selfish conditions. *For example*, saying "*If you do this, I will love you*" is conditional love. So if you don't do things the way your partner wants, their behaviour will change adversely. That is not love.

Similarly, if you agree to do things which they tell you to do (in their own selfish interest), then they will be affectionate towards you.

It is *"Relationship of Convenience"* and not love. Just introspect in your life and you will be able to think of at least few people that are having relationship of convenience with you. Probably you are too, doing that to someone. And let's not be judgmental, it is not a bad thing. Everyone has different equations with each other. When we don't know every detail about anyone's journey or circumstances in life completely, we should not blindly judge them. But one thing is for sure that relationship of convenience is always short term. Enjoy each other's company while you can because one day you will block each other for sure. So yes, it is alright if people are benefitted from such relationships, but it is not love. Does it mean there should be no conditions at all in love?

Is it even possible? The honest answer is that it is not possible. There can be conditions. Good and well - intended conditions.

For example- Your girlfriend/wife telling you, *"Do not drive too fast"* and if you do and she gets angry at you then probably this is love because her condition is <u>in your own interest</u> and not for any selfish purpose. She cares for you and that is why those conditions are completely valid in love.

Even a minute selfish interest at the cost of your partner is not love, for sure. It can be in mutual interest but not for opportunistic reasons.

To continue with the same *example*, if your partner is worried about your safety when you drive too fast <u>AND</u> also thinks about her own future (that she would be lonely without you), that is valid as well. There should be a win-win situation for both the parties concerned. But if one person is benefited at the cost of the other then it is not love.

Imagine your mother. They say that a mother's love is the purest form of love. She loves unconditionally and without thinking of her own interests. She sacrifices a lot for us. And that's the word which we shall use to understand love better- "<u>*Sacrifice*</u>".

Sacrifice is a hallmark of a genuine relationship. If you can sacrifice (in all practicality of course) for your partner, then probably you are in love. People who claim that love should not be *"practical"* and *"pragmatic"* are stupidly indulgent and self-harming pain glorifiers who end up regretting a lot, later in life.

It is very important to consider the pros and cons, have clear communication with your partner, constantly observe your equation, ask the tough questions and ensure that you are sacrificing for the right reasons.

And when your partner also sacrifices for you, then it becomes a successful relationship and an unshakeable trust is formed.

To give a very relevant example of the present times, many youngsters go abroad for further studies. Many relationships fall apart because generally people don't want to get into long distance relationships. Most people are not privileged enough to go abroad and visit their partners frequently. Moreover, there are lot of insecurities and trust issues. So, most of them break up. But I have seen the power of love and sacrifice. Two of my friends were in love and the female partner had the opportunity to go abroad. She decided to not go because she did not want to get separated from her partner. She rejected the scholarship to study in London, just to be with her lover in India! This is a big thing. To sacrifice your dreams just to be with the person you love. Many people would call this step *"regressive"*, especially when it is taken by a female. Probably it is. Probably not. Everyone has their own priorities. But guess what her partner did? He went on to convince her to take the scholarship and go and achieve greater heights. **This is love!** Both of them gave priority to each other's well-being before their own interest. The girl went abroad, they both had a roller coaster ride in their relationship but none of them gave up. Today, they are happily married and are going from strength to strength.

Always remember, the wrong ones will distract you from your goals but the right ones will always inspire, support and encourage you.

"Be with someone who brings out the best in you, motivates and supports you in achieving your goals and brings positivity in your life."

Anyway, enough of being too romantic. Let's get back to some reality. Love is not always blissful and fantastically happy. Love also brings some amount of pain and heartache which some of you might have already experienced. Sometimes, love is a quiet emotion that in time becomes the oxygen you need to breathe and any form of removal of it begins to choke you.

Moreover, actual love is when a person generates all types of emotions within you — emotions of love, affection and care and at the same time affect you in a way that you get irritated and angry at them.

Hypersensitivity occurs when you are in love. Your emotions flow uncontrollably and excessively. Everything gets multiplied by 10-15 times. Normal actions of your partner like replying late to your texts, missing your phone calls, forgetting important occasions, getting late for a date, bonding with the opposite sex and million other things which normally wouldn't bother you, hit a different nerve when you are in love.

Love and hate are the same train, only in forward or reverse gear. When you are in love, you are not the best version of yourself, you become extra sensitive and all the negative emotions like jealousy, anger etc. gets magnified.

Do you ever feel like *"I love this person but at the same time hate them for certain characteristics or traits which they possess"?* It can be anything from the way they talk/behave/dress/eat to their personality traits like being too possessive or demanding etc. If yes and you are still with them, congratulations...you love them. Heard this cliché line? *"Love is when you accept the person for who they are."* Well, it is true though. Let's dig deeper.

Nobody is perfect. We all are full of imperfections. Some have fewer flaws than others but nobody can say that they are completely flawless. If they do then they are deluded or probably too pompous. This brings me to our *third love test* which is, to accept your partner with all their flaws and weaknesses.

Now doesn't it sound quixotic and unreasonable? *For example*, imagine your partner being an alcoholic or a domestic abuser and you say, *"I love him for who he is and accept him with his flaws"*. It is bizarre and silly, right?

If yes, then what is with everything that romantic movies and novels have taught us? They did teach us to love unconditionally without changing the other person. Does it mean they were wrong?

Absolutely not. But they taught us at a very surface level. Sometimes, half knowledge can be dangerous.

So, to expand this brief about accepting flaws, let me connect this to the point we made in the *first love test* - about keeping your partner's interest before you.

So when your partner is trying to change you FOR YOUR OWN GOOD, don't counter them by giving this idealistic line about accepting your flaws and the way you are. They care for you and that is why they want to change your bad habits and flaws, for your own benefit. Or perhaps for the benefit of you both.

On the other hand, when they cannot accept you for your natural personality, it is not love. Just because they are not happy or comfortable with your personality, and they want to change you, don't give in and change yourself. But there is a very thin line of difference between the two and people often get confused. Let me give examples of both the situations.

First set of examples are about positive changes in your personality which your partner wants to bring, for your own growth.

Examples :-

1. Changing your unhealthy food habits and teaching you dining table etiquettes.

2. Changing your dressing sense <u>to make you look better</u>. *(Not to make themselves comfortable. So if your guy asks you not to wear short skirts because he is possessive, then it is his problem and not yours)*.

3. Changing your rash driving and other reckless habits.

4. Improving your hygiene and standard of living.

5. Grooming you, for your own benefit.

The above mentioned are just few examples of changing the person in a good way for their betterment.

However, harmless flaws and imperfections are beautiful. They make us who we are. They are an integral part of our identity and everybody has flaws and imperfections.

"A true relationship is two flawed people refusing to give up on each other."

Below mentioned are some examples of not being able to accept your partner for *who they are.*

Examples:-

1. Not being able to accept that their partner is too thin/ too fat/short in height/too many pimples etc.

2. Unable to accept their partner's original skin colour. *(Pressurizing them to use fairness creams and go through surgeries and skin lightening treatments)*

This happens a lot especially with girls. Somehow in our regressive society, dark skinned girls are not considered "pretty". How pathetic that is!

"Sadly in many parts of our country, intelligence is limited to talking in English and beauty is limited to having a fair skin."

3. Not being able to accept the nature of your partner. Emotional people are asked to be calm, angry people are misunderstood, shy people are forcibly instructed to talk more and misjudged as arrogant and friendly extroverts are asked to stay away and not make new friends.

4. Forcibly thrusting your habits like smoking or drinking onto your partner and if they refuse, then behaving unreasonably with them.

These are some of the habits of a person who tries to change their partner. The moment the partner does not give in to those unreasonable changes, the peace is shattered and these people fight, argue, do all kinds of drama and emotionally or physically cause damage to their partners. That's a toxic relationship, if you realize you are in one, just run and don't even look back. Some relationships can't be resuscitated.

"Find someone with whom you can completely be yourself without any hesitation."

Coming back to the opening line. "Love is overrated". Actually it is not. The stress and tension caused by being unaware about what love is, is overrated. The whole meaning of love is misunderstood these days. If you can identify whether what you have with someone is love or not, then you can easily sail through and form a successful relationship.

The problem today is that the idea of what is love is unclear in most of our minds. The three love tests mentioned in this chapter will guide you and make you understand whether you are actually in love or you just "think that you are in love".

These tests are not the only parameters to measure the existence of love or potential of a successful relationship. It may happen that all the love tests are fulfilled and yet things don't work out in a relationship due to other reasons.

It may also happen that two people are not in love but can still form a lifelong successful relationship and live happily with each other.

"The love tests are not mandatory but recommendatory in nature."

Love tests can help you to identify the reality of your love. It can make you aware about your current situation. If you introspect, many of you will realize that you are in a relationship but not in love. Some of you may find out that one of you is in love and the other is not. Few of you will discover that your relationship has the potential of being a successful relationship. Some lucky ones will be happy to realize that they are in love and the person they love also loves them back. The only thing I would like to add is that the "love tests" are not just one time tests.

They need to be observed and tested CONSISTENTLY.

You must have heard many couples say, "We fell out of love." This is because they were in love but were not consistent. Probably they unconditionally cared for their partners and put their partner's interest before themselves but could not do it long enough.

"Being consistent is extremely important to have a long lasting and successful relationship."

There will be good times and also terrible times. But if you both love each other, then don't give up during the bad phase. Hold each other's hand and sail through. Sadly, quitting is the easiest and most convenient option in present times.

If you want to quit then quit "trying to please everyone", "fearing change", "living in the past", "overthinking", "being afraid to be different", "self-doubt", "being directionless" and "giving up easily". However, never quit a happy relationship because of avoidable squabble.

During the COVID 19 pandemic, people are dying alone and are not even able to have a final conversation or a last hug with people they love. Even after witnessing such uncertainty of life, if you cannot let go of your ego and continue to fight over silly issues then there is something terribly wrong with you.

If you observe your own family closely, in most cases your grandparents and parents have had long successful marriages (yes, there were a lot of fights but they did not give up on each other). It is because that generation believed in repairing broken things. Our modern generation is the one that throws away things which are even minutely cracked or damaged. We are shrewder, impatient and less forgiving.

Therefore, when you find a beautiful romantic connection, test it whether it is love or not and if it is, then trust me you are one of the luckiest people because finding love is rare these days.

"Finding a partner is easy but finding love is certainly not."

So, when you are sure that there is love from both ends (it's alright if the intensity of love varies between the two, eventually it will get balanced), then don't ever give up because of inconsequential issues or ego clashes. Stop fighting with each other and start fighting for each other.

"Love is precious. Save it. Protect it. Cherish it."

CHAPTER 2

"THE NEGATIVE LIST"

Welcome to the second chapter folks. I hope you are engaged and involved in the content of this book. The writer and the reader share a very beautiful bond. We have never met or interacted before and now we are talking about some very personal things. The connection is just like a relationship where we gradually discover each other.

What? How?

Glad you asked.

You may be thinking it is just a one-way communication. Well, if you take it in literal sense then probably it is, but the way I see it...you are discovering yourself by reading it and indirectly I am discovering myself (because of you) by baring my soul and trying to express my thoughts which were perhaps not even known to me. For me, it works like a therapy where I can articulate what I feel about love, relationships, heartbreaks etc. and you can get a realistic perspective. A win-win situation for both of us. Cheers! So just hang in there and keep relating your life with the things you read, I am sure you will discover many new things and re-discover some already known stuff.

In the very first chapter we talked about what actually love is. Now I personally find it very risky to love someone. And let me tell you that we are talking about "LOVE" and not just casual dating or relationships with mere infatuation.

"Love is a serious business."

It is not just about *"having a good time"*. You sacrifice, you think about them before yourself and you blindly trust them. You are giving someone the power to completely break and destroy you and trusting them that they will not. This can be highly unpredictable and dangerous if you do it for the wrong person. Many lives have already been destroyed because of this. Many people become alcoholics, drug addicts, depressed, insane and suicidal when they fail in love.

I am sounding too worried and scared, right? You must be thinking that I am probably overreacting. Many people would say they move on easily. If they can do so, great. But most people cannot move on. Especially, when they have loved someone with all their heart and did not receive the same affection in return.

Some people are clever enough to constantly and minutely observe their relationship, their partner's behaviour and the changes their equation goes through.

These smart people come to know that their love is not being reciprocated or appreciated enough and the other person is not a compatible partner. So they may breakup or even if they don't because of any reason, they are aware that things are not the way they are supposed to be.

These perceptive people don't go through a lot of pain due to heartbreaks and can move on quickly after falling out with their partner. You all must have known some people like that. Probably you are one of them too. They are the ones who often warn you by asking *"Are you stupid enough to trust that guy/girl, again?"* or after a separation casually say *"It's okay, relationships break, people change, we need to move on."* How can they ever understand that not everyone is ready for a heartbreak or separation? For most of us, it comes as a shock. But these smartasses somehow predict what might happen and for them it is a normal phenomenon. I think we should appreciate such people because they do what everyone should do, that is to be "aware" and keep observing the minute changes in their relationship and their partner.

A perfectly compatible person few months ago might not be the same today. People constantly evolve with time and so do you. Love is not something that once tested, does not require any further observations. There needs to be constant checking and rechecking if you don't want to get that hazardous shock in the end. I am always amazed and impressed with people who can do that. Apart from being discerning and perspicacious, they are also practical and that is of utmost importance. When they feel things are not going right, they get detached.

This prevents them from having any emotional trauma because they have anticipated the problems and are already prepared for the worst. But not everyone is so clever, certainly not in love. Most of us lose our sense of objectivity when we are in love.

Moreover, regularly observing and testing is tiresome. It does not allow us to enjoy the guilty pleasure of getting indulgent in the ecstatic feeling of being in love. But the least you can do is to be sure that the person you love, loves you back!

Don't just fall in love because you want to or because you like the idea of "being in a relationship". In the previous chapter, we learnt about what actually love is. Now in this chapter we shall find out whether the person you love is the right person for you or not. Trust me, it is the most important thing. Even more important than love itself.

Doing everything unconditionally for a wrong person feels miserable. Trust me, I know.

So how do we know whether a person is right or not?

Well, there is no particular definition of the *"Right Person"* to fall in love with. A right person today may not be the same tomorrow. Also, who says that you get attracted to only the right person? You can fall in love with anyone, anytime anywhere. And that is the scary part.

So when there is no proper way to *"fall in love"* with the right person, one should at least know the traits of the wrong person.

Before we talk about the wrong person, I would like to make it very clear that we are talking about *"the wrong person to fall in love with or be in a serious romantic relationship with"*.

We are not judging them as individuals. We are only judging them as our partners. They are not bad people.

They are just not suitable to be in a relationship with. Make sure you understand the difference.

In many cases, these people are themselves not aware of their own toxic traits.

So what kind of people are we talking about? I call it *"The Negative List"*.

Let's list certain types of people in our Negative List, which you should avoid being in a relationship with if you are looking for love and a serious long term romance. If you are not, then probably you are with such people for your own benefits and that is fine too.

1. The Horny Type – No emotions only sex

These lustful people are only looking for physical intimacy. That is completely fine but only when two people are on the same page. Sex is great. But if they are looking for JUST that and you want a lot more from the relationship then trust me, you don't want to get involved with such people. The conflict will be that the priority and driving force of the relationship for you will be love or being together but for them, it will only be about satisfying their lust. They will only like you when you give them what they want. Your relationship will only be about physical intimacy and nothing more. They will not have anything more to offer and your relationship will lack depth and emotional bonding.

They might force you, threaten you and try to get physical without your consent. They will not care about your feelings or emotional needs.

There are high chances that they might switch to a more attractive partner and leave you with absolutely no explanation, it is called ghosting.

It often happens that after an intimate night either between strangers or known people, one person wakes up alone in the morning because the other person has already left and ghosted him/her. That's because they already got what they wanted and are not interested in anything further. Coming back to our topic, these kind of people frequently cheat on their partners whenever they get a chance. Now, Infidelity is a very complex thing. It has different scenarios and is also driven by circumstances. A whole chapter is dedicated to the topic of infidelity separately where we shall discuss it in detail, in the later part of the book.

Many people think it is mostly the guys who are hornier which is not always true, but they certainly express it much more than girls do.

Obviously, not all guys are motivated by their lust but we all have desires. Everybody needs physical intimacy and it is absolutely a normal thing. And these types of people include not just guys, there are girls who are looking for just physical intimacy and nothing else but are seldom able to express it openly like guys, because of the narrow, regressive mindset of our judgmental society and social stigma attached to a girl wanting to satisfy her desires. Let's not do moral policing and say being horny is bad. It is not.

Sex is one of the basic human needs. Both genders need it equally. However, what we are targeting here is wanting to only have sex in disguise of love and using someone who is unaware of your intentions to satisfy your lust. So, when two people want to have sexual relations and they are on the same page then it's their choice.

"Friends with Benefits" is already a hit concept all over the world. Two consenting adults can do whatever they want without any judgments or moral policing.

2. *The Narcissist*

Robert Downey Jr. as Tony Stark has somehow made this word sound cool. We proudly put out photos on social media with the caption *"Self Obsessed"*. We associate the term Narcissism with self-confidence and self-love but actually it has a different meaning altogether.

Narcissism is a disorder.

Some say it is a rare disorder but I think its symptoms are found very commonly. We all love ourselves and that is normal. However, when people do not think about anything else apart from their own self, then it is difficult to be with them. Signs of narcissism may include (and are not limited to) cold heartedness, superiority complex, grandiose self-image, entitlement, conceit, boundary violations, false charm, the Don Juan syndrome, manipulation, irresponsibility, rule breaking, extreme selfishness, negative emotions and contempt towards others.

Now what exactly narcissists would do? Simple. They will never accept their fault. Every relationship will have fights and arguments. No two people are completely same. They have different opinions and different ways of doing things.

Narcissists would only want things to be done their way. They have this unshakeable belief that whatever they say is right. If you oppose them, a lot of personal attacks will be hurled at you.

Whenever they make a mistake, they will not accept it. Even if they do, then somehow they will manipulate you into thinking that they committed the mistake because of you or they are being gracious by accepting their fault for your benefit and make you feel guilty. People of both the genders can be narcissist. Usually experts say that these people are *"suffering"* from this disorder but in reality, it is their partner who is actually suffering.

These people lack empathy. You may be emotionally hurt or broken but they will never understand that. They are just full of themselves. They will want you to do things they say, wear what they want, the food will be ordered as per their taste, holidays will be at the destinations which they prefer, your social circle would only consist of people they like, movie dates will only be about their choice of films and their timings etc. They will start controlling your life. They will behave as if they own you.

Everything should be just about them, is what they strongly believe in. They will make you feel inferior when you unintentionally commit even small mistakes. They will never shy away from telling you how fortunate you are to be with them. Their sexual desires will always prevail over yours. During your intimate sessions, even if you are not satisfied but if they are done in bed, then the show is over.

Such people are dangerous to be in love with because you will gradually start losing yourself. Your life and existence will be all about them (which would be a good thing in love if the same is reciprocated as well). Your self-confidence will be reduced drastically. If you want to save your self-respect and individuality, then stay away from the narcissist type.

3. The Gold Digger/Opportunist

These people come into your life for financial benefits. They see in you, an opportunity for them to grow financially or maintain a luxurious lifestyle. You may attract such people if you are rich, have a powerful position or probably have contacts or connections with wealthy and influential people. If you, yourself want to be somebody's sugar daddy or sugar mamma then it is your choice.

Then probably, you may get involved with such people and spend lavishly on them to get in return whatever you want. However, if you are looking for love and serious, long lasting romantic relationship then such people should be avoided at any cost (pun not intended). It is difficult to do so because these people are usually very charming.

They know how to woo people. They have the talent of saying the right things which you want to hear. They are extremely good at hiding their real intentions.

The best way to identify such people is to initially keep paying for your first few dates, buy expensive gifts for them, spend some bucks on them and just observe how they behave.

You will see a twinkle in their eyes when you do these things. They will try their best to hide it but their love for money and free stuff will clearly be noticeable and evident. If they dutch the bills, also buy gifts for you etc. it does NOT necessarily mean they are not gold diggers. They are probably very smart gold diggers who first want to gain your trust and then grab a big jackpot amount later. You need to keep testing them in order to make sure they are not gold diggers and opportunists.

Set a trap if you doubt their intentions. Tell them that you want to be independent and don't want your family wealth or tell them that you want to donate everything and start afresh. Then just sit back and carefully watch their reaction. If they take the bait and give out negative reactions like panic, anxiety, discomfort, nervousness, dismay, perturbation or fright, you will know their real intentions.

It's not bad to love money and wish for a luxurious life but the problem with falling in love with such people is that, their priority is not love. They might be a perfect match in terms of compatibility in the short run. There are high chances that they will possess all the qualities which you are looking for in your partner. But *"intention"* plays a vital role in a relationship.

"Why are they with you?" If the answer is not to unconditionally love you and is only about acquiring wealth through you, then the intention is not right for a long term relationship.

Once your money is gone then they will be gone too. The moment they find a richer person, they will replace you without slightest of hesitation.

4. The one who cannot get over their ex-lover

Such people do exist everywhere and I have all sympathies for them. Probably they were deeply in love with their former lover or perhaps, they still love them. These people cannot move on. They are either scarred for life or still waiting for their ex to get back in their lives. The problem with being in love/relationship with them is that they will try to find their former lover in you. They will subconsciously or sometimes intentionally compare you with their ex. The fights would normally have words like *"He was much better than you"*, *"She did not behave like this"*, *"He would not have talked to me like this"*, *"She cooked better"*, *"He understood me better and accepted me the way I was"*, *"We had such a beautiful connection, I wish he/she comes back"* etc. These people should be avoided mainly because during the bad phase (every relationship has good and bad phases) they will easily give up on you and often openly express their regret of breaking up with their ex. They will not miss a single chance to be in touch with their ex again or meet them (sometimes even secretly).

They will stalk their ex (even if their ex has moved on happily) on social media and keep talking about them all the time, even in your personal intimate time (which can get really annoying).

Another big issue is that their life can be controlled by their former lover. Their ex has a strong influence on them and can make them do anything! You have absolutely no control over them. They might go against you if their ex convinces them to. Your life is completely dependent on the intentions of their ex. If their ex chooses to create trouble, you cannot prevent it.

For example- If the former lover asks your partner to have a fling with them, such partners would easily do it without thinking twice. Just imagine how heart-breaking it will be for you if that happens.

Your partner might also provide their ex-lover with financial and other resources which were originally meant for you both. It is unreasonable for us to expect that if they loved someone and it did not work out, they should move on quickly.

We need to have some sympathy and give them time. Having said that, if they still cannot get over their ex (or probably they don't want to), in spite of all your efforts then there is nothing more you can do except leaving them for your own good. You also have a life after all. You also have some desires and expectations. You cannot waste your entire time waiting for them to get over their ex and keep spending your energy in convincing them to move on especially when there are no efforts from their side.

If you can tolerate their attachment with their ex-lover and be at peace with the fact that they can never get over them and move on in life, then you may get into a relationship with such people, at your own risk.

5. Alcoholics/Drug Addicts

Before completely writing them off, let's be more empathetic and think from their perspective. Nobody wants to become an Alcoholic or a Drug Addict. These people are usually the victims of circumstances. They might have lost someone, faced terrible situations (it may be financial crisis, physical or emotional abuses etc.) or are going through a trauma. They may have found solace in alcohol or drugs. Is it right? Who are we to judge? If you love someone who is an alcoholic or a drug addict, then you will obviously put all your efforts into changing their lifestyle. You would want to save them from their own destructive habits. And you should try your best to make sure that they conquer their addiction and become sober. Don't give up on them easily. They need you the most.

But if you have given your best and still your partner is not able to get over their addiction and chooses alcohol or drugs over you (and probably even over their own self) then you should not spoil your life further. This is a very sensitive issue because in most cases the person is not within his/her own control.

You cannot blame them directly for being addicts. But you need to draw a line. If their addiction causes regular fights and you face frequent abuses and trauma, then you need to leave them and move on.

These people will spend all their money on drugs or alcohol and will have no permanent jobs or a secure financial position.

They will be more of a burden on you and your family. Their frustration will result into frequent outbursts.

You might have to face embarrassing situations at public places due to their behaviour. If you genuinely care for them then the best you can do is to emotionally and financially support their treatment including their rehabilitation expense and medicines.

6. *The Possessive type*

We as human beings are very territorial. We don't like to share our favourite people with anyone else. Somehow, we want to be first in their priority list.

We care for them. We want them to be safe and happy. This feeling is called being *"Protective"*, which is a good feeling. It is different from being *"Possessive"*.

The Possessive type is the most common type in the negative list. These people cannot see their partner having a good time with someone else, especially with people of the opposite sex.

These people are highly sensitive to you having any friendly interaction with the opposite sex, it may be your childhood best friend, colleague at your workplace or even your college buddy.

The constant thoughts in their mind are about *"What if something sexual happens between them?"* or *"Why are they so close? Was there a history between them? Or is something going on right now between them?"* or *"What will happen if they get too close to each other?"* etc.

Possessive people will have constant suspicions about your intentions as well as the other person's. They will take the smallest of things out of context and fight with you over a third person. You may simply be friendly, courteous and civil with someone and such people will not be able to digest that. A normal friendly hug or a peck on cheek greeting to any person of the opposite sex can make them really uncomfortable. Even if an irrelevant person (a stranger or a distant colleague of yours or some mutual friend of your cousin you meet at a party) hits on you then your possessive partner will overreact, even if you don't respond to the person's attempt at being too friendly. These types of partners will blame you for things other people do to you. You being attractive and getting attention will also make them angry.

They will start dictating as to what you should wear and to whom you should talk. Your relationship with your friends, colleagues and family can be completely destroyed because of such people.

Some people get possessive because deep inside, they believe they don't deserve you or you are much above their standards. They want your life to only revolve around them. Possessive people have trust issues, insecurities and low self-confidence.

To be honest, we all want to save our partner from interacting with the wrong people who have malicious intentions.

However, it is better to directly communicate with your partner about your feelings and opinions about a certain person and if there is a good understanding between your partner and you, then they will surely understand.

The main difference between being protective and being possessive is that being protective is for the benefit of your partner (you want them to be safe and avoid wrong kind of people) whereas being possessive is for your own self (you want your partner to avoid people because their bonding makes you uncomfortable, jealous and insecure). A possessive person is uncomfortable with mostly everyone close to you whereas a protective person makes sure you avoid certain people who do not have good intentions.

Being in love/relationship with a possessive partner can be really tough. All your time will be spent on convincing them and proving yourself innocent. One of the most important ingredients for a strong relationship will be lacking. That is trust.

You will be humiliated all the time. Your character will constantly be questioned by your partner. You will be accused of infidelity. Your relationship will never be about you two; it will always be about other people. Your daily discussions will only involve third parties. You will regularly be instructed to avoid any friendly interaction with people of the opposite gender.

Your entire life will be spent on proving your innocence to them and completely avoiding any friendly human interaction with the opposite sex.

It will adversely affect your career, studies, professional relationships, friendships etc.

You might get into depression and lose your confidence if this continues for too long.

The last two types are not in the *"Must be avoided at any cost"* type. They may be great human beings. However, being in a relationship with them has various drawbacks.

7. The extremely career oriented type

These people are obsessed with their own careers, to a point that they don't even consider spending time with their own parents, friends or partner. Being ambitious is a good thing but not when it affects your personal relationships in an unfavorable way.

There is nothing wrong with being a career oriented person and creating an empire or identity of your own. The only problem with such people is that they don't know how to "balance" their personal and professional lives. Such people will give all their time only to their career. There are high chances that you are not even in their priority list. Life might get boring for you. They may forget your birthdays/anniversaries, you might have to wait for hours for them to show up at home, they will cancel your romantic dates/holidays/social obligations etc. if it clashes with their work schedule.

Another gentle reminder, such people are not bad people. Their priorities are different and everyone has the right to choose what they want to do with their lives.

They may end up being a CEO of a Multi-National Corporation or successfully launch their own business startup, but their personal lives might suffer.

If you are okay with less or no attention from your partner then you may be with them. Their work being the top most priority does not mean they don't love you.

They just love their career more, probably at the moment or maybe they will always love their career more than you. They want to focus completely on their work and have high ambitions. Either they lack time management skills or they intentionally choose to allot all of their time to their career. If you can accept their obsession with their career and understand things from their perspective, then you may go ahead and be with them.

8. People who cannot appreciate

This comes from a very personal space. I don't like people who cannot appreciate what others do for them. A simple *"Thank You"* can actually make someone's day. One of the most annoying things in a relationship is when your partner does not appreciate you (or does not appreciate you enough).

In most cases, these people are completely unaware of how much efforts their partner have put into various little things. In some cases, they are aware of things their partners do for them but they still don't acknowledge it. They simply take their partners for granted.

Being in a relationship with such people will not have a direct, substantial impact on you but will indirectly make you feel irritated and make you want to reduce your efforts into strengthening the relationship.

Your disappointment at their cold reactions towards your efforts will gradually accumulate and result into suppressed frustration. This is because irrespective of how many sacrifices you make for your partner, they will never appreciate it. You will feel that being with them is a thankless job.

No matter what you do to make them happy, your efforts will not be valued at all. You will start questioning yourself whether so much effort to make things work, is worth it or not. If this continues for long then you will get tired of not being appreciated and end up making wrong decisions.

You must have heard many times where a cheating wife tells her husband and refers to the other guy by saying, *"He makes me feel like a woman. He appreciates my beauty"* or *"I wanted to feel loved."* This is a classic example of not appreciating the beauty and femininity of your girlfriend/wife and its consequences. We are not taking any sides here. If someone does not appreciate your beauty then cheating on them is also not correct. But sadly, this is what happens in most cases.

Appreciating is not just limited to beauty. It also means to make someone feel that you admire and value their efforts in everything they do to make you feel happy.

It may be cooking a meal of your choice, driving you to work or college, buying you gifts, planning a surprise birthday party for you, giving you important advices etc.

"Appreciate even the little things people do for you. It makes them want to give more."

Avoid being in a relationship with people who are ungrateful. They will not value anything you do for them. They probably will not even value that you are in their life. Once you leave them, then perhaps they might understand what they lost. Some would still not care.

The best thing you can do is learn to stop putting efforts for someone who is completely okay with losing you.

"Even the universe will give you what you want, if you appreciate it for the good things that you already have. Do not take things for granted. Nobody is obliged to do anything for you. Still if they do things for you, respect that."

So folks, these are some types of people which you might want to avoid if you are looking for a long lasting, happy, committed and satisfying relationship. In case you have not found your partner yet, then these points might help you in deciding what type of persons should be avoided. However, it might happen that you are already in a relationship with a someone who falls in the negative list.

In that case, talk to them, discuss the issues you have with them and give them some time to work on their shortcomings. Nobody is perfect. We all have our flaws.

"There is no Black or White when it comes to humans, we all operate in the Grey."

The fact is that many of us already have few traits of the negative list. The problem starts when your flaws get out of your own control and also create problems for your partner. This is where one should draw a line and start working on their limitations.

So dear readers, just because your partner is in the negative list at the moment, does not necessarily mean that you should leave them instantly. Give them some time to work on themself and be supportive.

Be their guiding force, stay by their side. Always remember this statement:-

"The wrong person will find excuses to leave but the right person will find a reason to stay."

However, one should also be pragmatic and sensibly realistic. Therefore, if you don't see things changing anytime soon and there are no efforts from your partner's side to work on themself then it's time to move on, for your own good. You may want to still stick with them because you are habituated with their presence in your life. You might have already invested a lot of time and energy in your relationship. You might want to be with them even at the cost of your own future. You might want to give them more chances in spite of knowing very well that things will not change, which shows how kind and generous you are.

Love is a strange thing, in spite of knowing how someone can damage you emotionally, break your heart, abuse you physically and emotionally and completely destroy your future, yet you still want to be with them because you are in love with them or you feel you cannot live without them. If you are one of those people who can take bullshit regularly from your partner just because you love them or want to be with them, then you are ignorant, stupid and very brave. I am not here to tell you what you should do with your life.

I am just here to show you the reality and then you get to decide your actions accordingly. Your future is in your hands and you always dictate how others treat you.

So friends, in my opinion if you really want to cherish the *"supercalifragilisticexpialidocious"* (yes that's a word) experience of *"being in love"* which you all have probably just heard or read about, then being in a relationship with the right person is of utmost importance. There is nothing like a perfect relationship. There will always be ups and downs in every relationship. There will also be a lot of problems, difficult situations, fights etc. All you have to do is find somebody who is worth all the sufferings and who firmly stands by your side during tough times or at least doesn't give up on you. Find a heart that will love you at your worst and arms that will hold you at your weakest. The right person will make you *"feel"* love and you will know that how marvelous being in love is. You will feel like your heart has finally found a home.

Therefore, be patient and don't settle for someone who doesn't deserve you simply out of desperation, fear of being alone or to follow a trend of being in relationships.

"There is no bigger regret than putting all your efforts and sacrificing everything for the wrong person. It is wise to save your feelings for someone who genuinely cares."

CHAPTER 3

"RECIPE FOR A LONG LASTING RELATIONSHIP"

It's 2 am right now as I am writing this chapter. I am hungry. Normally, at this hour I like to have some snacks. My mind is occupied with food at the moment, which will reflect in the content of this chapter a bit. So as the title states, you want to know the secret *"recipe"* for a long lasting relationship?

Well, you have come to the right place. Let me *"serve"* you what you seek.

To begin with, the most basic thing is *"willingness"* of two people to be together which makes their relationship strong. There will be many ups and downs, a lot of fights, misunderstandings, ego clashes and much more. If two people don't want to stay together, they will find many excuses and reasons to break off. However, if they genuinely want to stay together, no reason can separate them. Love is like cooking, we need a lot of ingredients to prepare a delicious meal.

Similarly, many things have to come together for a long lasting, blissful and satisfying relationship.

Secondly, like every other thing in the world, even love has got its advantages and disadvantages. Everybody wants to enjoy the highs but seldom people want to face the lows.

Interestingly, there is no standard list of advantages and disadvantages; everybody has their own unique issues.

For example- Rudy is unhappy because he is not getting constant attention from his partner Sophie. Rudy feels lonely and ignored most of the time. Harry also faces lack of too much attention from his partner Sandy but he doesn't think of it as a disadvantage. He likes this trait about Sandy that she gives him a lot of space and privacy. He is happy and satisfied.

If you minutely introspect in your life, you will find your own advantages and disadvantages.

"The point is to not get afraid or cautious of the disadvantages of love, but to find someone worth facing all the disadvantages."

The next most important thing to have a strong relationship is to never let things get boring. Do not let the charm of romance fade away. Make your partner feel special. I know it sounds too unrealistic as eventually things will get monotonous in all relationships. However, small gestures (depending on every individual and their choices as not everybody loves to get flowers, chocolates or expensive gifts) can really make a difference and can help you in maintaining a strong bond with your partner.

We are often quick to express our dislike or criticize our partner but seldom do we appreciate and compliment them for the good things.

Love and food are so similar, both are essential for our survival, we crave for it, when we have it we enjoy it for a while and then take it for granted and don't value it enough until we stop getting it and then finally we want it again! Therefore, always appreciate your partner for everything they do for you.

Little things like — helping each other in terms of work, sharing responsibilities equally, complimenting them often and always expressing how much you love them, can make your partner feel special. If your partner is important to you then SHOW THEM and make them feel valued.

> *"Touch them, even when your hands cannot reach them."*

Spend time together regularly. It can be a movie date, dinner/lunch date or as simple as going together for a walk. Be together and create more and more memories. Have at least one meal together. Talk before going to bed and share your daily experiences, feelings and thoughts.

Trust me, conversations at night, brings two people closer and increases emotional attachment. Real romance is when memories are created and it only happens when something special happens, something which excites you, where you get goosebumps, your heartbeats are racing, your face has a wide smile and your eyes twinkle with enthusiasm. For people who are married, the dating should continue even after your marriage.

Keep the excitement and adventure alive. Write love letters, hold hands, say *"I love you"* whenever you get a chance, life is short and the future is uncertain. Enjoy the present and your partner's company to the fullest. When love grows cold, recollect and relive the memories that ignited the fire of passion and adventure. Also, it is extremely important to be *"flexible"* and adapt to changes in your relationship in order to evolve as individuals and as partners.

One of the most vital things in a relationship is *"privacy"* of both the individuals. Some people like to share everything with their partners, some don't and it is completely alright. I have never really admired the concept of sharing passwords of your social media accounts with your partner or regular checking text messages of each other. It is absolutely necessary that an individual should be given some privacy by their partner. If someone doesn't share every minute detail about their life with you, it doesn't mean they don't love you. It's like we love our parents but do they know every private thing about us? No, yet we love them. There might be some irrelevant information which an individual might not consider necessary to share. Even if one of the partner shares everything and the other does not, then also it is all cool.

Don't break into anybody's privacy, otherwise they will start hiding things from you and that might not end well. Two people require absolute trust and understanding when it comes to privacy. Nobody should hide any important piece of information from their partner.

The definition of important information varies from person to person but overall it is something which can directly or indirectly affect you, your partner or your relationship.

An *"essential ingredient"* for a long lasting relationship is to be loyal to your partner. Infidelity is a very complex issue and a separate chapter is dedicated for it.

For now, just know that if you love someone, being faithful is easy. Don't fall into the trap of temptations and distractions for temporary pleasure; otherwise you will ruin a beautiful and rare equation.

Another absolute necessity is to be honest and transparent. Be it about your feelings, thoughts, inner battles and demons or your opinions. On a lighter note, if she asks whether she is looking fat or not, guys are allowed to lie. Many times, honesty can easily be misinterpreted as being mean or rude. It all depends on how you express yourself. If you don't like a gift which your partner has got you, you cannot be blunt and say that it is trash. You need to respect their feelings as well as their self-respect and yet be honest so that they don't repeat the same thing again. You need to explain them your reasons in a very gentle and polite tone so that they can understand. Listen to each other's point of view, recognize when the argument is going off the track and make the necessary repairs. Very often people get into arguments and fights not because of the difference of opinion but because of the tone of communication. It is very important that the tone of expressing is correct.

Even if you speak the *"truth"* but your tone is rude, then the other person will definitely get offended or hurt. It is important to keep your tone in check.

Many times *"honest people"* take extreme pride in their characteristic of always speaking the truth unapologetically and unabashedly but forget that they sometimes cross the line and become nasty, disrespectful and insensitive.

"Honesty does not have to necessarily be mean and hurtful."

A right thing said in a wrong tone can be really dangerous since the person who has said the right thing will be adamant that his/her point is correct whereas the partner would have forgotten the main issue and would have got offended by the tone of the speaker. Now both of them will think they are right and the argument will turn into a fight and clash of egos.

Ego is really a deal breaker. We all have it and we all have suffered or lost something because of our egos. It is extremely necessary to keep your ego flexible and do certain creative adjustments in a relationship. Ego clashes and bad behaviour have resulted into more break-ups than any other issue. Your heart decides who you want in your life but your behaviour decides who stays. I know that when our egos are satisfied, we feel very elevated and enjoy a sense of triumph but it is a very temporary feeling. The long term impact of it is always negative. It is impossible to keep your ego in check all the time but one should put constant efforts to do so.

When your partner realizes that you are putting efforts in controlling your ego, they will do the same for you. Lose your ego for your love but never lose your love for your ego. Having said this, it is even more important to keep your self-respect intact in any relationship.

"Do not lose yourself in order to keep your partner happy."

If your self-respect is high, your partner will also respect you.

Respecting your partner is an essential ingredient for a healthy relationship. You have to respect your partner, even if they are not doing well financially or emotionally. Respect should never be equated with success, financial background, caste or qualification of a person.

Respect should come from how a person is, how pure their heart is, how they treat others including your family/elders, how well-intended their thoughts are, how they treat under-privileged people, how they behave privately and publicly, how well do they handle difficult situations, how do they treat you in a relationship and how important role do they play in your equation. Trust me, the most romantic thing you can do for your partner is *respect them*.

If there is mutual respect in a relationship, a lot of small ego clashes and silly fights will be avoided.

People often fight over things like who is putting more efforts and who is simply not participating. There should never be one-sided efforts.

Relationships are worth fighting for, but you can't be the only one fighting. Some relationships succeed because they are destined to but most succeed because they are determined to.

Great things can never be achieved easily; you both will have to consistently work on it. It is vital that both the partners never stop putting efforts to improve their relationship and to make each other happy and satisfied. Once a person is convinced that their partner is putting efforts, they will automatically put equal or perhaps more efforts.

One of the *"secret recipes"* to have tranquility in your relationship is making peace with your partner's past. Everyone has a past. Some are grateful for a good time, some are grateful for a good lesson, some are ashamed of it, some are proud of it but it is extremely important to own it and be honest about it especially with your partner. Your partner should know the details of your past relationships and affairs, at what stage of your relationship you share it is your choice depending on the right time according to you. One should never hide things from their partner, they deserve to know everything.

"Honesty" and *"transparency"* are indispensable for success of any kind of relationship. You cannot say that your partner needs to know only those things which have happened after they came into your life. Only if they know and accept you with your past, they have truly accepted you. Some people might have had a very happening past with various flings.

If you think you haven't done anything wrong and it was all your choice (some mistakes as well), then own it up. If you have a dark and traumatic past, still you need to share it with your partner and make them understand the circumstances and your experiences honestly. In either case it is your responsibility to help your partner understand your past. You cannot expect them to immediately not react, but if they are mature and sensible people, they will gradually be comfortable with your past. It is a mutual understanding. *For example*- A person who has had a very colourful past cannot expect their partner to not momentarily judge them unless they have the same personality but if that person convinces them of his/her loyalty and is honest in their relationship then the partner will gradually come to terms with the past life and a strong sense of trust will be formed. It is very convenient to hide your past but it is not the right thing to do.

Another example is a more serious issue; many people (of both the genders) have been molested or sexually abused in their childhood.

These people have gone through a lot of emotional trauma and have suffered it alone. In most cases, they have not confided to anyone because of notions about the judgments they will face from their close ones and the society. Many times, their own family must have brushed the issue under the carpet and didn't stand up for them. Such people naturally behave a certain way; they have hostile reactions towards anything which reminds them of that incident and are very vulnerable to expressing themselves confidently.

It is the responsibility of their partner to be *"empathetic"*, patiently listen to them with an open mind, understand them, support them and get them out of that trauma. Always remember friends, when someone talks about their problems, you DO NOT talk about yours. You listen.

Coming back to the topic, disclosing your past to your partner is of great significance. It will help you create a strong bond with them. The best way to be in a relationship is being *"best friends"* with your partner.

"Sooner or later the attraction part will fade away but love, respect, care and friendship will always stay."

Share everything about your past with your partner just the way you would share it with your best friend. It is not as easy as it sounds. Your mind will give you a thousand reasons to hide it from your partner *("It will ruin things.", "What does my past have to do with my present or future?", "What difference can he/she make after learning my past?", "It will make him/her uncomfortable.", "He/she will judge me.", "Past is past, one should forget it.", "Even he/she must have had past.")* but it is really important to let them know in order to make them understand what kind of person you were, your thought process, what all you have experienced and how has it impacted and shaped your present personality.

As a receiving partner it is equally important to listen carefully and not to judge or come to quick conclusions when your partner honestly shares their past with you.

If you don't like the things you hear about what they did in their past life, don't react negatively.

When people confess something or share a traumatic experience, they are hyper sensitive as they are re-living that experience while sharing it with you.

Anything you say can deeply affect them so be patient, kind and make sure you don't react aggressively in a way which ruffles them and discourage or prevent them from honestly sharing their experiences with anyone ever again.

If they confess to making mistakes, they are already feeling guilty and terrible about themselves, make them comfortable and be their support and help them to be at peace. It is your responsibility to understand their mind set and appreciate their honesty. Not many people confess or share their past details. If you are receptive and simply listen to them when they are talking their heart out, they will be comfortable with sharing everything with you and being completely themselves around you. It is also your responsibility to keep their secrets and confessions *"highly confidential"*. Whatever personal things they share, DO NOT gossip it with your friends or relatives, keep it between you both only.

When you taste a food item and you find it too spicy/ too sweet/bitter/over-burnt etc. what do you do? You give your feedback to the person who has cooked for you so that in future the same mistake is not repeated and they know your opinion and taste. Similarly, in relationships the most important thing to do regularly is to COMMUNICATE.

It sounds very simple but most people fail to do so and gradually their relationship falls apart and they grow distant from their partners. Once the communication fails, everything else follows.

"Too much silence always has a deleterious effect on relationships."

It is also true that in a compatible and understanding relationship, both the partners are comfortable in each other's silence (not too much of it, obviously). *For example-* there is no need to constantly talk, sometimes two people can be together and do their own thing. When you two are in your bedroom, it's not always necessary to interact, it can happen that you are reading a book and your partner is working on their laptop. It is the presence of each other that matters and not constant interaction. However, if your partner has done or said anything that bothers you then express yourself and communicate with them.

The step which most people neglect during communication is to communicate in an understandable, polite, respectful and considerate manner.

Don't expect them to directly read your mind; you need to convey your emotions. Your partner needs to know which things bother or upset you so that they can avoid doing those things in future or at least give you their perspective and reason for doing those things. If your opinions are not communicated effectively then things will only get worse. Moreover, there can be times when staying silent momentarily might save your relationship especially during a heated argument or a big fight.

In such cases, you expressing your heightened negative emotions will make things worse, but make sure once everything cools down, you communicate your point of view to your partner.

"The best relationships are when yesterday's fight does not stop today's communication."

Similarly, when something has made you happy, it is your responsibility to communicate, appreciate and be grateful so that more of that will come your way in future. Your partner will also feel valued and will double their effort to ensure that you are content and happy. Don't take anything for granted. Every little thing your partner does for you is worth acknowledging. Have gratitude for one another. Also, regularly give honest feedbacks to your partner on what they lack and where can they improve, ask them what they want and expect from you and vice versa, discuss the traits you both admire and dislike about each other, talk about your future plans etc. Communication is the key to a successful relationship.

While writing this chapter, I received a message from my childhood friend Rajesh and his wife Priya. They had a huge fight over a meal. Now to just give you a brief background of my friends, Rajesh is an excellent Chef and he regularly cooks at their place while his wife is the Head of Finance Department in a reputed organization. She usually comes home late. Their fight was basically regarding the dinner cooked by Rajesh.

So what happened was that Rajesh knew that his wife was dieting and trying to lose weight since six months, so he laboriously prepared Russian salad, boiled vegetable curry and rice with low fat yogurt. Priya came home late from work and was extremely hungry.

She wanted to have delicious six course dinner! She was also going through her periods and she had craving for desserts as well, but none of it was available. She was disappointed and did not eat the dinner cooked by Rajesh and instead ordered food from a local restaurant. Rajesh was disappointed and got angry. She got angry at her husband as well, for making tasteless food and a huge fight erupted. The reason for this unnecessary fight was that both the partners were not on the same page, did not communicate properly and were impatient with each other.

Your relationship can go for a toss if both of you are not on the same page. *For example*, if one partner is thinking about marriage and the other is thinking about just dating, or one wants romance and the other wants a fling or one aims for unconditional love with passion and sacrifice and the other desires a convenient relationship involving wealth, lifestyle and social status, then things will surely fall apart quickly. Your partner and you should know about your expectations from each other (keep your expectations reasonable and realistic).

In today's day and age, we judge people and situations more vehemently and react instantly. We show apathy when we have to show kindness and we never really have the time to deal with anything disdainful.

We want everything instantly and hence have become intolerant to slightest of things which are outside the scope of our expectations. Patience in a relationship is the test of endurance and character. When we talk about patience, just relate it to any food item.

When we visit a restaurant, why don't they give us the food immediately after we order it?

It is because delicious meals take longer time to get cooked. We enjoy anything that is cooked slowly at low temperature. We also prefer ripe fruits over raw ones. Similarly, it is very important to have patience in your relationship in order to fully enjoy the *"fruits"* of it over a period of time. Being patient shows your loved one that you value them and your relationship enough to see beyond their faults.

By making yourself open to what your partner brings to the relationship, it shows that you appreciate their virtues. Showing your partner more patience can also inspire them to be more patient with you.

Good relationships don't just happen. Good relationships are built. They are nurtured. Patience may be a bitter thing, but the fruit of it is always sweet.

We all love food. We all have our favourite cuisine. Some eat to live and some live to eat. But imagine your life if you are told that since you love food, your each and every decision, opinion, feeling, desire and action should revolve around food only. You should leave everything else and just focus on your favourite food 24*7. Sounds terrible, right?

Suddenly, now you don't love your favourite food as much. Similarly, to have a long lasting relationship it is important to have a life beyond your relationship. Your partner is an integral (and perhaps the most important) part of your life but not your entire life. You were not born exclusively for them. You need to have your own individuality, have your own group of friends, desires, hobbies, goals etc. If you rely on your partner to fulfill you, it can lead to an over-dependent relationship where you stop growing as an individual. Your partner should be someone who makes you happy, but they should not be the sole source of your happiness. They should be a source of true happiness. So, make sure you nurture your own interests and desires, take a class you are interested in, make plans with friends and do things you love instead of waiting for your partner to fill in the void.

Don't fall for the so called romantic line *"You complete me"*. No! Nobody needs to complete anyone. Partners in a healthy relationship should *"complement,"* not *"complete"* each other.

Another common trend that I have witnessed recently is that most relationships fail because people want their partners to get them out of the stress caused exclusively by their own decisions. They want their partners to make them happy but they forget that happiness is always in their own hands. Just like a meal cannot be spicy, sweet, salty, bitter and sour at the same time, you cannot get all-in one partner without any limitations. We want our chosen one to offer stability, safety, predictability and dependability.

And we want that very same person to supply awe, mystery, adventure and risk. We expect comfort and edge, familiarity and novelty, continuity and surprise.

It's too much to ask for from one relationship! Therefore, if you want to have a long lasting and blissful relationship then it is not wise to put all the burden of your stress, happiness, expectations etc. on your partner.

One of the most essential ingredients for a long lasting successful relationship is the use of the three magical words, no...not *"I love you"* but – *Please, Sorry and Thank you.* These are perhaps the most neglected words in the world we live in.

It is absolutely bizarre that when we are close to someone, be it a friend or a family member, we forget our courtesy, chivalry, thoughtfulness and manners. Never stop using these magic words. When you want a favour or something from your partner, say *"Please"*.

When you have committed a mistake (sometimes you might not even realize), immediately apologize. When you are wrong, do not remind your partner of their mistakes which they committed in the past or keep arguing about how you "never intended" to make a mistake. When your partner tells you that you hurt them, you don't get to decide that you didn't. Just say *"Sorry"* and mean it. Saving your relationship is more important than pampering your ego.

Say *"Thank you"*, whenever your partner does something which is good for you or anything that you asked them to do. Such little gestures make a lot of difference.

It may happen that when you use such words, your partner may brush it off with a laugh, act like *"oh no need to say this"* or not respond openly but secretly they will admire you.

When you visit a restaurant with your partner, imagine how boring it would get if you both ordered exactly the same dish, every time? Variety is the spice of life and it applies to your relationship as well. We are not looking for our clones! It is important to have differences in your personalities to balance things and make it exciting otherwise if you both are exactly the same then what's the point of two people? One is enough.

Two different personalities blending together will enable you both to have an exciting relationship where you both will be able to get out of your comfort zones and grow as individuals. Therefore, always appreciate the similarities and respect the differences.

Being in a relationship is not just about dating, physical intimacy or finding a support system for your convenience, it is about being with someone who makes you happy in a way that nobody else can. A great relationship doesn't happen because of the love you had in the beginning, but how well you continue building love until the end.

It will never be *"perfect"* but make it work. It's worth it, trust me.

A successful relationship requires you to fall in love multiple times but with the same person at different point of time.

I am sure if you genuinely want to be with someone, you will find solutions to every problem and this recipe for a long lasting relationship will enable you to have a romance that people often say doesn't exist anymore.

"Relationship is not just about loving your partner today or tomorrow but is about loving them every single day, every single minute and every single second."

CHAPTER 4

"SHATTERING MYTHS"

For all of us who have grown up on a steady diet of cheesy romantic movies and lovey-dovey scenes on daily soap dramas, we tend to hold a lot of mistaken beliefs about relationships. What appears all fun and games on the screen actually takes a fair amount of work in reality. Let's shatter few myths that you may be consciously or sub-consciously holding on to.

The first reality check which you need is to basically understand that relationships are not easy and effortless. Love is tricky, beautiful and messy at the same time. We all come with emotional baggage, personality flaws and several other issues which can hinder our relationship if constant efforts are not made to make things work. We cannot say that god has already made our pair with someone in heaven and all we have to do is just meet them. This belief not only creates unrealistic expectations about relationships but also generates fear and anxiety inside us about never finding *"the one."* Also, just the one? Out of billions!? I don't believe in the concept of just one soul mate.

I believe that we have multiple soul mates and the one with whom we end up with depends on how evolved our soul is at that particular juncture of our life. There is a soul mate at every stage of our life. As we grow, so does the quality of our soul mate.

Even when you find your soul mate and your relationship might seem like a fairytale romance initially but if committed hard work is not put then it can soon turn into a catastrophic nightmare. In fact, what I believe is that more than fairytale, it is the "real" part of a romance which is magnificent.

Eradicating our expectations of a fairytale love story is important to appreciate the true beauty of our romantic relationships.

If you randomly ask people to name few qualities which they want in their partners, the most common answer would be honesty. Most people consider lying a deal breaker. They think that if their partner lied to them means they are dishonest and not trustworthy, but that is not always true. The main point is to know their "intention" for lying. If the lie is to manipulate or hide important facts then it should be a deal breaker.

However, lies can be of two types - *"White lies and Black lies"*.

Black lies include deceiving your partner for personal selfish gains. White lies are innocent lies which are told to avoid unnecessary fights or arguments and to keep things smooth and healthy.

Examples of a White lie would be *"Hey that cake was delicious"* but in reality it tasted like shit but you surely don't want to hurt your partner's sentiments or discourage him/her from baking or *"You look so amazing in that shirt"* because sometimes complimenting your partner is necessary to make them feel confident. Therefore, it is a myth that occasional lying is a serious crime and is a deal-breaker. Only the black lies are deal breakers.

Another myth which I find absurd is thinking that it is absolutely necessary to play *"mind games"* with your potential partner to make them fall in love, to attract them or to make them realize their love for you. Another gem from pop culture.

We have all inevitably listened to friends, relatives or silly movies and books which teach us that playing certain mind games is necessary to make someone fall in love with you or to keep your relationship strong by grabbing your partner's attention by using such tricks.

Examples of such silly mind games and their sillier reasons include:-

• Not replying to his/her texts immediately.

(Reason - they will think you were desperately waiting for their messages/ they will think you are too free, unoccupied and easily available).

• Not to sound too interested and act as if you are *"too cool to bother"*.

(Reason - If you don't do this, they won't value you enough/they will take you for granted).

- Let them put more efforts.

(Reason - If you put all the efforts and don't let them put any effort, you will lose your importance and they will become complacent/ chances are that they won't value your extra efforts because they will think this is normal).

- Play hard to get.

(Reason - they will think you are too easy to get and nobody gets excited when things are easily available. Moreover, we have this mentality that *"people want what they can't have"*. Not always true).

- Exaggerate and over hype your desirability. Show them that a lot of people want you.

(Reason - This will make them compete and put much more efforts, give you undivided attention and be available for you all the time just to prevent you from going out with anyone else).

However, the fact is that all these silly tricks work only in the short run or don't work at all.

The only thing these tricks and mind games result into is completely turning off the person you want to attract. Avoid using these tricks and mind games. Trust me, nothing works better than being completely yourself and honestly expressing your feelings. If you can't stop smiling or blushing on seeing someone, then please don't. It's okay. Don't control your natural emotions and try to hold back. Let them know how they make you feel. Don't try to be someone else to attract people, be exactly the way you are and the right kind of people will get attracted towards you. Don't bother how the person that you like will perceive you or how desperate, clingy or needy you may sound.

If you have feelings for someone then instead of playing these games, express yourself wholeheartedly. It works like magic!

"Anything spoken or felt honestly from your heart will surely touch their heart."

Another thing that many movies have taught us is that, making your partner jealous gets you more attention. Balderdash! We are also convinced that jealousy and possessiveness are desirable qualities in your significant other. If they don't get possessive about you around others, it must mean that they probably don't love you. Wrong! It's high time we recognized that possessiveness and jealousy are unhealthy feelings and we need to view them as red flags in a dysfunctional relationship. True love is built on mutual respect and trust, and a lack of these values can drive a couple apart eventually. Sadly, we use it as a tool to attract people. While men and women are just as likely to experience jealousy, their reactions differ. Men either get very defensive, angry, irritated while women feel uncomfortable, distant or will get completely put off, lose interest and believe that the relationship isn't worth it. However, all these are just statistics and observations. Such gender stereotypes may not always be true as it all depends on the individual characteristics. One of the biggest myths among the youth is that making their partner or potential partner jealous is a shortcut to getting instant attention from them.

It only works in the short run and mostly has a very negative impact. You will surely get attention but that won't be what you expect. Trying to make your partner jealous can backfire.

So, kindly don't do the following to make your partner/potential partner "jealous" :-

•   Unnecessarily praise/compliment a person of the opposite sex in front of them intentionally to make them jealous.

•   Stay online and chat with others instead of replying to their texts and purposely making them wait, just to artificially ignite a sense of craving inside them, for you.

•   Going on dates with others to make your potential partner jealous and wrongly thinking that they will realize their love for you after seeing you with someone else and openly express it or make the first move.

All these things don't work at all. It will not only put off your partner or the person whose attention you want but also using someone else for your selfish motive can create complex situations.

Let me give you an *example* to show you how complicated situations may arise due to the silly idea of making a person jealous in order to attract them.

In our *example,* the story is that Alia loves Kabir and wants his attention. She wants Kabir to put an effort and make the first move.

Kabir likes Alia as well but he doesn't express it openly nor does he do anything extra-ordinary as per Alia's expectations. Alia has a classmate named John.

Alia decides to use John to make Kabir jealous, so she starts flirting with John, holds his hand in front of Kabir, asks him for movie and dinner dates in a way that Kabir notices etc.

Kabir gets envious. John is unaware of Alia's intentions. Alia is successful in her mission to make Kabir jealous.

Now what?

The best thing that can happen is Kabir confesses his love for Alia and Alia accepts it just like she had planned and then explains the whole situation to John, who has no other choice but to accept the reality.

However, many complex versions can be created due to Alia's actions :-

•	John gets attached to Alia and starts having real feelings for her.

•	While using him, Alia falls in love with John and realizes that he is a better guy for her than Kabir.

•	Alia gets Kabir to propose her which she accepts. John realizes that he was being used and decides to take revenge.

•	Kabir thinks Alia is not trustworthy and won't be a loyal partner. He never talks to her again.

•	Kabir and John end up fighting for Alia and someone gets critically injured or worse!

•   Kabir decides to settle scores and starts having an affair with another girl, leaving Alia heartbroken.

Hence, instead of playing such mind games and making people jealous, just go to them directly and express your feelings honestly.

Before continuing, I would like to narrate an incident.

I went to hang out with some of my friends. One guy was showing off how he got laid with a stranger he met randomly. He was constantly bragging about how smooth he was and how he impressed the girl. I was simply listening to him and observing his body language and also of my fellow friends. Unlike me, they all were impressed and in awe of him.

Then that guy continued and started boasting about how many girls he has been with. I feel all this information is supposed to be private if not for your own sake then at least for the girl. Respect her privacy!

At the most you may share your experiences with your best friend or someone whom you are close to. However, boasting of your sexual encounters, dates, affairs and relationships publicly is plain stupid. If your girlfriend or boyfriend sends you their private pictures on your request, look at them and delete them afterwards, or at least don't flaunt those pictures in front of your friends just to get some praises or project yourself as an achiever.

This incident made me realize about another myth - More romantic/sexual partners means more success/bigger achievements is what many idiots strongly believe.

I have seen a lot of people unnecessarily bragging about it as if they have won some award or a Nobel Prize. Dude, you just got laid, that's it. You didn't do anything out of the world. You may think that you impressed the other person but probably they wanted the same thing and they might have led you on and attracted you. You may like to believe that you got what you wanted from them but there could be a possibility that they "had you" instead of "you having them". Unfortunately, boasting about the number of sexual encounters and affairs give many people more self-confidence and pampers their fragile egos. The myth is not just internal but also how externally people perceive such people. Most people also get impressed and believe that if you have multiple affairs and sexual encounters, you are achievers, cool, attractive and desirable.

The issue with these "players" is that they treat humans like objects. They have no value for anybody's feelings or emotions. They believe this is a game and they are players who simply want to play and win. For them, winning is getting laid or manipulating somebody do things which they want them to do.

Without sounding too rigid and traditional, the fact is that having multiple partners makes a person unable to settle down with one individual. You get habituated to live like animals, mating every time you get attracted to anyone.

If you continue to have casual affairs and multiple sexual partners for too long, it will be very hard (pun not intended) for you to commit and stay loyal to one person and be satisfied with them. This is a psychological fact. You will be habituated to having multiple partners. It's like an addiction. You will not like to get committed or get attached to just one person. Even if that one person is attached to you, you will shy away from being too expressive and emotional with them. In your mind you would have concluded that having emotions is a sign of weakness. You will forever be stuck in the never ending cycle of changing partners and will never be able to settle down. You can easily become commitment phobic.

So, it is wise to not let the perception of a "wild life" or sayings like *"Life is short, enjoy it with as many people as you can"* or *"If half of our lives are spent in sleeping at night, then why to sleep alone?"* get to you and force you into the world where at the end you wouldn't be able to feel love for one person and everything would simply be about physical intimacy with multiple partners. This myth is just like a teenage myth where teenagers think smoking makes them look "cool" but in fact it is injurious to health. Similarly, this myth of believing that having multiple partners and having a wild sex life is cool can be injurious to your love life and mental health.

Don't get me wrong. I am not preaching that you should only have one partner in your entire life. It is impossible in the world we live in. I am also not saying that if you have multiple partners in your life then you are a bad person or your character is questionable.

Some people may rightly say that they don't have multiple partners out of choice but due to failure of past relationships or simply because they have not yet found the right person.

However, the issue is not with having multiple partners over a period of time but with people who think that having various sexual encounters and affairs is a "cool thing" and they considered themselves as skilled and desirable. This kind of mind-set can be termed as "shallow thinking" and ultimately that person will never be able to experience love, honesty, stability and loyalty.

People who say things like *"God has created so many attractive people, why to settle with just one?"* and *"If you can get it why resist it?"* will someday understand that all this is just momentary pleasure and the real pleasure is to be with that one person whom you love.

"There is no better love making than one with feelings."

Another myth about love is that it binds you and your life should revolve around just one person. It is also a wrong perception that love creates a lot of boundaries and makes you feel caged. It is not necessary that all your important life decisions should be based on your partner's consent or should resonate with their lifestyle or merge with their opinions. A long lasting relationship is when both the partners give space to each other to fulfill their ambitions, desires, achieve their goals and supports each other in every situation. Love does not bind, it liberates.

Few days back at my office, I heard one of my female co-workers cursing one of my guy friends. I asked her what was the issue and she said that she loves him but that stupid guy doesn't make the first move. She actually said this, *"I am waiting for him to ask me out so that I can say yes to him."*

This is a very common scenario — a guy and a girl are in love, they both know it, and their friends know it as well. Everyone can feel the romantic tension between them. They both also know how compatible they are and how bright their future can be together. Still somehow it is always expected that the guy should start off the conversation.

Now, this is a very stupid yet a very common myth. It is often believed by the masses that a guy should always make the first move otherwise people will question his manliness.

The traditional male dominant and patriarchal society gives all the rights and powers to men. Therefore, even the right to make the first move which is now more of a responsibility is thrust upon the guy. There needs to be more cases where a guy and a girl really like each other and the girl makes the first move to which the guy simply respods. It's completely fine if a girl takes the initiative, the guy will not become less of a man. Too many responsibilities are unnecessarily thrust upon guys. Some of them are :-

- To initiate the first conversation,

- To ask her out on dates and pay the bill as well,

- To pick and drop her home,

- To open doors and pull chair for her,

- To kneel down and propose to her.

A guy can love his girl and yet may not follow any of these stereotypes and it is completely fine.

Guys who willingly do such things out of chivalry are great though, brownie points to them. But if you are a girl and you like a guy who would not make the first move then simply make the first move yourself! Don't play by the old patriarchal rules set by the outdated society. Take control in your own hands. Start the first conversation, ask him out and propose to him first if you really like him. There is no rule that only a particular gender has the right to express themselves first or have the responsibility to make the first move and continue to lead the equation in their own direction. A woman who approaches a man stands out, and we can determine a few things about her. Her bold, no-holds-barred approach tells us that she is confident, spontaneous, brave, outgoing, direct and thinks outside the box. All of these are attractive qualities in a woman; they make you appear humble and real. You should never hinder your chances and opportunities by thinking you are too good to approach a man or assume that he knows you are attracted to him.

One of my best friends broke up with her boyfriend. Do you want to know the reason? No, he didn't cheat on her or abused or misbehaved.

She broke up because as per their "zodiac signs", their future wasn't bright enough and their compatibility as per some zodiac compatibility check on Google was just 26%.

Hey don't judge my best friend…alone! Let's all judge her together. I mean how stupid can you be to ruin a beautiful equation based on zodiac signs and applications.

Another compatibility test showed 93% when they entered their details again in a different app! Finally, they are back together because they understood that such tests on the internet should not be taken too seriously.

There are 8 billion people in this whole damn world. People cannot be categorized into just 12 types. It is quite silly to check emotional, sexual, social compatibilities with your partner or potential partner via zodiac signs. Kindly don't burden your equation with these complex things which you don't even completely understand. There can be a possibility that some of the things mentioned in your zodiac sign are true for your personality but never follow it blindly and make important decisions based on that. I know a couple who had 90% compatibility as per their zodiac signs and they broke up in just a week and I also know a couple who had 23% compatibility but are happily together since many years. Zodiac signs are not individualized and specific all the time. Signs do hold truth in certain traits people born under them will have, but everyone is an individual and utilizes their traits differently. Love is a spiritual connection, it supersedes all signs.

There is no standard formula to judge either a person or your relationship through zodiac signs. It all depends on the individuals and the compatibility varies from couple to couple. You can have a bad relationship with a compatible sign and vice versa because signs don't guarantee that your partner will not cheat on you or will not lie to you.

Zodiac compatibility might help you to find someone with a few similar or compatible traits but as we have learned in chapter three that a long lasting relationship requires much more. It is better to listen to your heart rather than believing the planetary positions.

The issue is not with the science of Astrology at all. It has worked successfully for many people, has saved many from various harmful situations and also improved their quality of life.

But it is important to get such advices in detail from an authentic source and also to be logical and practical about it.

There are many things that we don't understand, so we should neither blindly follow them nor disrespect them. It is important to have a balanced and holistic view. I believe in destiny but I also believe in karma. Yes, everything is already written before you were even born but it doesn't stay the same. Every action you take and the choices you make in your present, defines your future. So even if you are destined to be a billionaire but if you spend unnecessarily on random things and don't invest or save your money then it will be gone.

Similarly, even if your destiny or your horoscope says that you will get a wonderful partner, but if you don't take care of your partner and put required efforts in your relationship then soon they will be gone too. Moreover, God has given us intelligence. It means we can adapt and change as per our wish. We evolve. So if you justify some of your flaws and bad qualities with your zodiac sign then you are being an idiot.

You cannot say, "I am short tempered because I am an Aries!" That is atrocious. Don't take your zodiac signs so seriously that you end up reducing your scope of growth and narrowing your horizons.

While coming back from work, I randomly heard a guy telling his girlfriend, "Stop talking to any other guy", the girl was stunned but she must have loved him so she simply agreed. Then he went further and ordered, "Don't even like any guy's photo on social media".

The girl simply nodded. The guy then must have felt guilty and awkward so he said, "Even I won't talk to any other girl except you."

I don't intend to judge anyone based on their personal equations but I feel there is a myth that once you are in a relationship, you should stop talking to the opposite gender or stop making new friends. This is more of a constant dilemma than a myth which many people face after getting into a relationship. Ideally, there are always boundaries which cannot be crossed, like you cannot go on a "date" with another person if you are already committed nor you can flirt openly with other guys/girls or hook up with them (unless you are in an open relationship).

You need to keep your new friendships very pure, platonic and have some boundaries.

Many times, couples keep fighting or feel insecure if their partner meets a person of the opposite sex, especially for a one on one interaction at a café or some private place or have to travel together for work purpose. Some people even have a problem when their partners indulge in regular texts/phone calls with anyone.

Some rigid minds are really not open to their partners making new friends. Some people tolerate such unreasonable demands of their partners just to be at peace and to avoid fights in their relationship, some don't. It is vital that partners have a strong sense of trust between them and are totally secure about themselves and their connection. You need to give space to your partner to make new friends irrespective of the gender. However, you must have heard common stories of people cheating on their partners with the new equations they form or probably even with their partner's best friends or relatives. Does this mean no new equations shall be formed at all?

Well no, meeting new people is a good thing. You should make new connections and friendships. It will help you grow and evolve as an individual. Nevertheless, if your new friend or acquaintance is misusing your friendliness by unnecessary flirting, getting way too personal or making constant passes at you, then it is equally important to keep observing them, maintaining some distance, expressing your displeasure and asking them to back off.

It is also a myth that being silent or ignoring unwanted attention is the best way to avoid any awkward situation. If you ignore their passes and do not address it, they will think that you don't mind the attention and will continue to do so which will not just make you uncomfortable but your partner as well.

There are many such desperate people who if not prevented, can mistake your silence as consent. They must be given a serious message that their behaviour is not appreciated.

Ultimately in order to make progress, develop your personality, widen your horizons, it is of utmost importance to regularly meet new people. Some of them can become really close friends or some may be essential for your professional growth and networking. Therefore, one cannot (and should not) stop making new equations simply because they get into a relationship.

Also, one should not remain silent if they are getting unwanted attention which makes them uncomfortable. Voice your thoughts fearlessly.

A myth that has ruined many relationships is that if you are deeply in love and have found the *"right person"* then you won't have any fights.

There can never be any relationship where there are no fights or heated arguments. Many people break their relationship when there are few occasional fights thinking that their connection is weak or their partner is not *"the one"*. The fact is that having fights is not an issue, but what ruins a relationship is not resolving your fights.

Productive conflicts that help the relationship end with *"some mutual decision about how to manage the disagreement"* are necessary. However, physical and emotional abuses, nasty, scornful or condescending fights that leave couples resolution-less and not talking for days can damage the relationship. The right thing to do during or after a fight is to approach the issue calmly and with clarity, and work on a constructive solution.

Frequently, accepting the difference of opinions and positively concluding healthy arguments give a couple a strong sense of trust and confidence that they can withstand any number of conflicts together.

A common myth among people is that if they are in love or in a relationship, they should be together and madly in love all the time, 24×7!

It is an insanely suffocative expectation of people to be inseparable all the time. Spending time on your own hobbies, with your own friends and family, or pursuing your own goals is extremely important. There is so much to be gained and enjoyed during time spent alone or apart. Also, I strongly believe that absence really does make the heart grow fonder. You need to miss your partner occasionally in order to have a high level of excitement when you meet them. There needs to be some amount of longing for each other in order to keep you involved and interested in your partner and your relationship. A bit of absence also makes a person realize the value of their partner in their life.

Another silly and unnatural myth is that if you are in a relationship, you cannot get attracted to anyone else. How is it even possible?

Any straight guy will obviously get attracted to a beautiful girl and vice versa. Why just limit it to straight people? Anyone can get attracted to anyone irrespective of the fact whether they are in a relationship or not.

The more important thing to focus on is — what one does with that attraction.

If they *"act upon"* it by cheating on their partner or flirting uncontrollably then it is wrong. However, if anyone gets attracted to a third person and simply admires him/her harmlessly then nothing wrong in that. It's completely normal. If you keep restrictions on your partner to even feel basic human emotions (which is honestly beyond their control) then they will start hiding their feelings from you in order to avoid confrontations. It's best to be open about your partner getting attracted to anyone else, allowing them to share their thought with you, tease them, joke with them, laugh over it and move on happily.

One myth which I find very common among the youth is that they believe love should be *"crazy"* and full of excitement all the time. I have known people who would say things like, *"If you truly love me, you will jump off the building for me"* and then when the partner is just about to jump, they will stop them and believe their partner actually loves them. I mean what a stupid narrative to believe in the first place.

The one who is asking to do crazy things in the name of love is mentally unstable and so is the person who actually does these crazy things to prove their love. Another conversation that I heard was during the COVID-19 Pandemic, which shocked and irked me. One girl asked her boyfriend to meet her on her birthday in spite of the lockdown. She said that she doesn't care what the situation is, she wants to spend her day with him or else she would break up with him because according to her — if he doesn't meet her on her birthday, he *"doesn't care"* and *"doesn't put efforts"* in their relationship.

I find it extremely unreasonable to emotionally blackmail your partner into doing things which can harm them. The guy broke the rules and went to meet her to prove his love for her and got infected with the Corona virus while travelling — they came into close contact and ultimately both of them got infected!

"Love means thinking of each other's safety and saying no when it needs to be said."

Genius is about knowing when to stop. Love does not mean that you simply agree whatever your partner tells you to do. You cannot claim to love your partner just because *"you do everything they ask you to do"*, *"you agree to everything they say"* or *"you provide them with everything they ask for"*.

You may disagree with your partner on several things like career paths and choices, major purchases, religion, politics and more. Disagreeing is not a sign of incompatibility unless you want it to be.

A mature relationship is when both partners have different opinions and yet listen and try to understand each other's point of view. There shouldn't be any force or emotional blackmail to make your partner do anything which they don't believe in. Therefore, one should stop doing crazy things just to forcefully make things exciting and "fun" all the time!

It is a myth that if you love someone, the passion and attraction will never fade away. The bitter truth is that passion naturally diminishes in all relationships.

The early days of a relationship are marked by excitement, fluttery hearts, butterflies in your stomach, sparks flying, and passions running high. As the responsibilities grow and roles expand, couples have less and less time and energy for each other. It is not a bad thing. Many people panic when they stop feeling that *"spark"*, not sensing that it has been replaced by a more profound and longer lasting version of comfort, love and affection. You can reignite that spark over and over, but with time love changes and grows with us. We must embrace these changes if we want to experience the depth of a long-lasting relationship. It might happen that the sexual activities might reduce as time passes by and it's completely fine. Sexual needs vary from person to person as well as across relationships. It is not the number of times you have sex, but the fulfillment you get with each other that matters.

A couple's romantic life is intensely private and must be motivated by their mutual satisfaction, rather than parameters prescribed by society.

What we fail to realize is that a stable relationship involves much less fluttering and breathlessness. As affection deepens, our love grows stronger for each other.

The spark is still there, and it can be reignited with attention and fresh energy. If you keep harping on excitement and novelty, you will miss out on growing together with someone and experiencing the best of a romantic relationship. Somehow, our generation doesn't like when things are *"normal"* because we believe being normal is monotonous and boring.

Sometimes, silence and calmness is also an integral part of love. It is wise to have a basic awareness that you both will not always be excited all the time in your relationship, no one is. Learn to be satisfied with the *"calmness"* and *"silence"* and simply co-exist peacefully.

Myths hold powerful control over our lives. When we let them govern the way we view and behave in our relationships, we are inviting unnecessary difficulties that prevent us from being happy. Instead of struggling to conform to an external definition of an ideal relationship, it is much better to tune into an authentic version of your relationship using internal cues. A foundation built on *"your own"* reality is going to make a far healthier and happier relationship than any myths and fantasies that you could create about a perfect partner.

Chapter 5

"COMMON CONFLICTS"

No relationship is complete without conflicts, they are inevitable. If you are not fighting or arguing over issues, then you are not completely involved in your relationship. If everything in your equation is going very smooth, happy, peaceful and you and your partner agree to everything you say to each other then surely something is wrong. People get angry and are willing to spend their time and energy on explaining their point only when they actually care about the other person's opinion. Anger, irritation, jealousy and all such negative emotions are off springs of love. If I love someone then only I will spend my time and energy on making them understand my perspective. Only if I love someone, their words or actions will actually affect me. Only if I love someone, I will argue or fight with them beyond a point. Only if I love someone, I will pursue them and try to convince them even at the cost of my ego. More love and care results into that person affecting you emotionally at a much quicker rate than anything else.

If you closely observe your life, you will realize that you experience a strange kind of sadness and anger when you have fights with someone you love, be it your partner, your friends or your parents. They can bring out the deepest of emotions within you. You might be getting angry at a lot of things and you may get irritated by a lot of people but people you love hit a different nerve which can really bother and annoy you. Having said this, occasional conflicts, fights and arguments is a sign of affinity.

It is a good thing to have conflicts, but in limits. If you have constant conflicts over every small issue then something is wrong in your relationship and you need to address the same.

Doing tasks with someone and succeeding together creates a strong connection. Similarly, when two people fight, argue and then solve the problem together, they get closer to each other and their bond gets stronger. However, there are some conflicts that can ruin your relationship and it is absolutely necessary to avoid them or quickly solve them.

What causes conflicts?

It is our habits and traits.

Let's discuss them one by one.

I know many couples who get into lengthy tiresome fights because none of them are able to accept their mistake. They are rigid and adamant that they are right and the other person is wrong.

Seldom have we humans accepted our own mistakes especially when it is pointed out by someone else. A situation can occur where one person commits a mistake (be it small or big) and their partner reacts depending on their patience level or the effect of the mistake on them. Now if the person does not accept his/her mistake or is oblivious to his/her blunders, then it causes a lot of heated arguments in a relationship.

This conflict can be avoided if one simply introspects and admits their mistake without any ego. Admit your mistake, apologize and move on! Constant unnecessary arguments can make things worse. The suffering partner also has the responsibility to make the blunderer understand their mistake and properly explain to them what went wrong and its impact on their relationship. It is vital for the partner to not react too aggressively or in a way that will prevent a person from admitting their mistakes in future. Having said that, it is equally important to be firm and make sure the same "avoidable mistakes" are not repeated.

To people who have committed some mistake in a relationship intentionally or unintentionally, own up to your mistakes.

Don't ever be that type of a person who doesn't admit his/her mistake and gets angry because their partner reacted to their mistake. It is simple; you committed a mistake, so bear the consequences and your partner's wrath (unless it includes violence or abuse). You have absolutely no right to get angry at them for being angry at you.

If you have ever behaved badly after committing mistakes and your partner has still forgiven you, or you are not with that person anymore because you broke up with them for reacting to your mistake, then immediately apologize to them after reading this and be at peace.

There can be several conflicts in a relationship. Every single individual is different from another and when two individuals come together, there can be a lot of clashes.

The common conflicts in a relationship are mostly as follows:-

1. Ego Clash

As identified in the earlier chapter, ego clash is one of the most common conflicts between individuals. Often people are not even aware when they mess up because of their egos. Some people are way too proud of themselves and have overtly high self-esteem and because of that toxic self-importance, they often directly or indirectly humiliate their partner and make them feel inferior. They may be immensely proud of their looks, wealth, education, family background etc. They have a very high level of superiority complex and because of that they will never take their partner's consent, advice or even consult them before taking any crucial decision which can affect the entire relationship. Egoistic people often need and want *"complete control"* over everything, even at the cost of their partner.

Such toxic behaviour is intolerable and it is better to give them constant reality checks and if that backfires and creates more issues then it is better to leave them for good.

However, there are some people who keep up with all the negative traits of a person they love and consider it as their own destiny and continue to get dominated and humiliated and lose their self-respect for their love. Each to his own, we can neither make a choice on their behalf nor we should judge them for their tolerance and submissiveness. I personally don't recommend tolerating negativity beyond a point.

It is very easy to choose between right and wrong but very difficult to choose when both the parties are right in their own way. Sometimes, ego clashes happen not because of one toxic person, but because of two strong minded individuals who don't wish to give up on their stand.

Both of them are completely convinced that they are right and don't want to surrender or even compromise. This situation often leads to stretching of fights, constant arguments and high level of aggressive behaviour between two people. It can be smallest of things but due to ego clashes it turns into a big clash. Mostly, all human beings overreact in the battle of egos. A person may do something which their partner may not like, then their partner will overreact to their mistake and then they will overreact to their partner's overreaction and it will all blow out of proportion. Ego clashes are tricky because they are messy, but it happens all the time because relationships are messy. Let's take a small *example* of two partners — David and Leena.

David doesn't listen to Leena when she tells him to wear formal clothes for a party. Now, Leena is upset but still David wears casual clothes of his choice.

The next day, they are going to meet David's parents. David asks Leena to wear the dress which was gifted to her by David's mother in order to make his mother feel good.

However, Leena has incidence of the previous night in her mind about David not listening to her regarding his clothing at the party. So now, Leena also decides to not take David's suggestion and wears what she likes.

To understand how alarming the situation can get, let's elaborate further.

While they are driving to visit David's parent, Leena asks David to change the music but he ignores her because he doesn't want to do what Leena says (because she didn't listen to him about her clothes). Leena asks David to take a halt. She wants to freshen up and eat some snacks as she is hungry. David refuses to do so because he is still sulking and now both are upset. Leena decides to text back a guy from her workplace who she was ignoring as he constantly kept on flirting with her since past few days. The guy replies quickly and starts flirting again and Leena enjoys the attention she gets from him, especially in that bad mood. This bothers David further and now he starts getting weird thoughts. He tells her to stop talking to that guy. Leena tells him to mind his own business and not to interfere in her personal life. David angrily demands her not to go to that workplace anymore. Leena yells back and they begin to quarrel. Both of them start reminding each other of their past mistakes.

Things get worse. Finally, they reach and both are in a terrible mood. Leena greets David's parents very coldly as she is already in a bad mood and she cannot fake her emotions. David's parents start to dislike and judge Leena. Now things get really messed up as David accuses Leena of infidelity and disrespecting his parents while Leena blames him for being immature, stubborn and insensitive.

Both are correct in their own ways and yet both are wrong. Different people have different perspectives, for some David may be right for some Leena may be right.

Some may blame David for being the cause of the whole scenario while some may blame Leena for involving a third person into their relationship. A small issue of not wearing outfit as per your partner's choice has now intensified, magnified and gone out of control.

Therefore, it is best to avoid ego clashes by — giving up unnecessary control, respecting the other person, trusting them, thinking from their perspective, forgiving small mistakes, learning to let go, being honest with each other and not keeping any kind of negativity in your mind and heart. Always try to keep your ego in check.

"Keep your self-respect intact but your ego flexible."

2.   *Involving an outsider*

When two people have any issues, they both need to sort it out themselves. Have a relationship where you can sit down and dissect your issues, sort them out and maturely come to a win-win situation.

It is very difficult to execute that, but that is the only proper way to conclude any issue. However, we are often dependent on others to solve our problems. Normally, mutual friends or relatives make a couple sit down and sort things between them. It may work for some couples but I personally don't recommend this. I would like one of the partners to be a bigger person and approach the other to discuss the issue and the other person should positively respond as well. Discuss and understand, simple.

Sometimes involving another person, irrespective of how close they are to you, can create more problems than you can imagine.

Let's continue with our previous *example.*

Leena and David are not on talking terms since few hours after the incidence in the previous example. They are behaving very oddly which makes David's parents uncomfortable. With good intentions, they talk to them at dinner table and ask them to sort things out.

David ignores his parents but when Leena shows her lack of interest in sorting things out, David thinks she is again behaving coldly with his parents and not responding to them properly. David now starts to say rubbish things to Leena which deeply affects and hurts her. She leaves the dining table and goes to her room and cries. David leaves as well. Both are hurt.

David feels bad for his mother who had prepared his favourite food so he comes down and eats it while Leena cries to sleep, without eating anything.

David sees his mother doing the dishes alone and judges Leena for not even helping his mother. The next day, Leena's mother calls her and Leena shares her grief with her but also admits that to some extent it was her fault as well. Her mother asks Leena to give the phone to David as she wants to convey to David how much Leena loves him and has admitted her part of the mistake to her. However, David has in mind that Leena didn't respond to his mother's request of sorting things and had left the dinner table and also didn't help his mother in cleaning the dishes. So, David clearly tells Leena that he doesn't want to talk to Leena's mother. Now Leena's mother and Leena think David is being rude and unreasonable as she only wanted to sort things between them. Everything is a mess and now both Leena and David don't respect each other and have a situation where they have to choose between their parents and their partners. Leena doesn't appreciate David not talking to her mother even out of courtesy and angrily leaves while David thinks she gave up on him so easily. He also starts having suspicions about the guy at her office.

Therefore, to avoid such situations it is better to not involve any third person as it will indirectly pity them against one of the partner whom they do not favour.

There can also be situations where you share your relationship issues with a friend of the opposite sex, who may have a crush on you or is attracted to you.

They may even dislike your partner for various reasons – they are jealous of your partner, they are unhappy and frustrated because they have not found the right partner for themselves, may be they are your best friend and are territorial about you and want you all by themselves, perhaps they feel that they have become a second priority for you due to your relationship etc. Therefore, many times people you confide to about your fights with your partner, try to create more distance between you and your partner and instigate you further to fight more by giving all sorts of wrong advices. Hence, two people should always sort out their problems with maturity and patience instead of involving any other person. It is important to not let opinions and biases of other people affect your relationship.

3.   The third person

There is always that one person whom you don't like but your partner is really close to.

It may be your partner's best friend or a relative. You just don't like their vibe. It's not even jealousy at times. You just naturally cringe when your partner is enjoying their company.

You may have expressed your dislike for that person and yet your partner tries to convince you that, he/she is a good person and you are the one who doesn't understand them or you have a prejudice against them.

It is completely fine. You don't have to like all your partner's friends and relatives.

As long as an outsider (however close friend or a relative he/she is) doesn't adversely affect your relationship or create problems for you both, it is okay to let your partner enjoy their company. It is not necessary that your partner and you will like the same type of people. Both of you have the right to choose your own company (as long as they are not toxic and harmful).

If you think your partner is in a bad company then explain your point to them in detail and make them understand. However, instead of discussing, most people fight and argue over others.

"Often the cause of arguments in a relationship is a third person. It is not wise to give an outsider so much importance."

4.   *Personal choices and habits*

A lot of conflicts occur because of bad decision making by any partner which affects the whole relationship.

For example:- Bad financial decision by one partner like investing in stocks and losing money which adversely affects the entire relationship as their savings is lost, from which they had planned to buy a house. Drinking and smoking habits of one person affects the whole relationship when health of that person deteriorates and a lot of energy, time, money and other resources are spent to save that person from an easily avoidable situation.

People, who have a habit of drinking too much regularly, often physically abuse their partner which causes them mental and emotional trauma.

Day to day decisions like where to buy a house, where to work, when to throw a party, where to book a hotel, where to travel, when to attend an event etc. are some decisions which if not taken properly and are not mutually decided by both the partners, can lead to highly volatile and ugly situations. If something affects both the partners, decision should not be taken by just one of them without consulting the other partner.

5.   *Unreasonable expectations*

Most people have unreasonable expectations from their partners which their partners are unable to fulfill. This causes frustration, anger, dissatisfaction and a lot of other issues. It is absolutely normal to not always get what you want.

Your partner may not be in a position to fulfill your expectations and demands. It is very common for people to burden their relationship with a lot of expectations and desires.

If your expectations are fulfilled, new expectations will be formed. Human wants and desires are unlimited and keep on multiplying. Also, in the age of social media it is very common to compare your life with others and feel dissatisfied.

For example - You expect your partner to take you out for dinners frequently because your sister's boyfriend takes her out every alternate day for dinner at five star restaurants or, you expect your wife's parents to gift you something expensive because you have witnessed your best friend getting extravagant gifts from his partner's parents.

This can create a lot of conflicts in a relationship because when the expectations are not fulfilled there will be disappointments, blame games, unpleasantness, constant fights and personal attacks. Of course, there are some exceptions to this. *For example*, someone who reacts violently when angry should be expected to learn to control their violent reactions. But in general, you need to accept your partner, for who they are.

Both the partners need to be very realistic, pragmatic and should not let unreasonable expectations ruin their relationship.

6.   *Changes*

I find it amusing when people break a relationship by giving reasons like, *"He/She just changed.", "He/she isn't the person I used to love anymore.", "He/She has become a completely new person.", "I wonder whether I actually ever knew him/her."*

It is impossible that people remain constant throughout their lives. One needs to accept the fact that it is natural that people change and evolve with time. You need to understand that with different experiences, achieving milestones, facing challenges in life, both of you will change as people. It is extremely important to support who your partner is rather than expecting them to forever remain as you would like them to be.

The true test of your relationship would be if instead of conflicting over changes, both of you accept that you have evolved over time and fall in love with each other's new personalities.

You will realize that over a period of time, you have been in a relationship with many personalities all combined in just one person!

Adapting to changes is important to survive. Arguably, even the mighty Dinosaurs that ruled the Earth for approximately 165 million years around 65.5 million years back couldn't survive because of their failure to adapt to rapidly changing climatic conditions.

Embracing an open mindset that allows for change and being willing to adjust and adapt creates space for your relationship to evolve with it.

CHAPTER 6

"INFIDELITY"

Infidelity has existed since commitment was invented, yet this extremely common act remains poorly understood. Around the globe, the responses I get when I mention infidelity range from bitter condemnation to resigned acceptance to cautious compassion to outright enthusiasm. In some places, the topic is a dining table conversation, while in my hometown, a group of women seem to view their husbands' philandering as unfortunate but inevitable. In metro cities, some women proudly see the rise of female affairs as a form of social rebellion against a chauvinistic culture. Infidelity may be ubiquitous, but the way we make meaning of it—how we define it, experience it and talk about it depends on our personal choice and upbringing.

Infidelity can be a deal breaker in a relationship for majority of the people. Isn't it the worst thing your partner can do? How can they cheat on you? Did they forget all the promises? Don't they love you anymore?

Well, infidelity is not as simple as it sounds. It is everywhere, growing rapidly and becoming common with each passing day.

"Infidelity can happen in bad relationships as well as in good relationships."

Unfortunately, people have no understanding these days on how to handle infidelity. There cannot be screaming, shouting, violence or an impulsive decision.

Firstly, one needs to give the cheating partner an opportunity of being heard. Listen to them why they cheated. Also, try to understand the difference between cheating and being unfaithful.

Most people use this term interchangeably but there is a difference. Cheating is when you indulge in any sexual activity with anyone outside your romantic relationship. Unfaithfulness is a broader term and it involves not just sexual activities but also emotional detachment from your partner. For many people cheating can be a forgivable act but being unfaithful should always have serious repercussions as it also indicates that there is something majorly wrong in your relationship. However, the damage that infidelity causes the aggrieved partner is just one side of the story. To know the real reason behind infidelity it is of utmost importance to hold the cheating partner accountable and ask for a proper explanation. The cheating partner must admit what happened, give adequate reason for their action and take full responsibility.

If you have cheated on your partner then you must be completely transparent and provide honest answers to all the questions being thrown at you. This will lead to conversations about what went wrong and what needs to change. Then the ball is in your partner's court. They may forgive you and continue with the relationship or they may dump you. It's completely their choice, not yours. You have already committed a wrong action, now leave the fate of your relationship in their hands and face the consequences. Most people that I know have forgiven their partners. A few of them have got separated as well and some weirdos have asked for one sexual encounter with another person just to *"settle scores"*. They be like, *"You had one affair outside our relationship, so I should get to have one as well…take it or leave it."* It's a power which they have earned because of their partner's infidelity.

But personally speaking, this is a stupid thing to do. One cannot compare and keep an account of bad things their partners do and do the same things to settle scores.

Infidelity needs to be understood in detail. It can be of two types - *physical and emotional.*

Emotional infidelity describes relationships that break the boundaries of exclusive relationships but are not sexual or physical. An emotional affair generally starts innocently enough as a friendship.

Through investing emotional energy and time with "a friend" outside a committed romantic relationship, the platonic friendship can begin to form a strong emotional bond which hurts the intimacy of the current romantic relationship.

Emotional infidelity is more dangerous for a relationship since one person is not emotionally connected or involved anymore. It causes emotional distance and detachment in a relationship. Your partner going on movie dates, dinners, holidays, trips, events etc. with someone else, sharing their personal feelings with them constantly about everything and making future plans with them is part of emotional infidelity. It touches upon the issue of unfaithfulness. It means your partner is not as emotionally connected to you as much as they are with someone else. Just because your partner didn't get physically intimate with the other person does not mean they are faithful towards you. You can argue that a person can share every personal thing with their best friend as well. However, a best friend is not someone with whom you make future plans to settle down romantically or lie to your partner about meeting them regularly and making a connection secretly behind your partner's back. In emotional infidelity, there is a complete lack of *"emotional investment"* of your partner in your relationship.

Physical infidelity is terribly wrong as well. It typically means engaging in sexual or romantic relations with a person other than your partner. However, that doesn't mean that the partner who cheated doesn't love you anymore or they are toxic people.

If they are repeated offenders then you need to end things for good. However, if they have confessed to falling in the *"lust trap"* and losing control, try to empathize with them. Their guilt is already killing them.

You still have the right to end things and it is also completely fine because nobody can say things *"just happened"* because everything is a choice.

In taking a dual perspective on such an inflammatory subject, my personal advice would be that if you are in a long, intense, romantic relationship or marriage where you have found *"the one"* and everything seems perfect to you…and if unfortunately your partner has succumbed to desires and temptations (and he/she is not a repeat offender), confesses it to you immediately and is extremely guilty and promises not to repeat the same mistake again, then it is wise to accept it, move on and continue with your amazing relationship.

Everyone makes mistakes; it is important how one handles it. If your partner confesses in a dignified and apologetic manner and is feeling sorry of their action and ensures you that they won't repeat this mistake ever again, then trust me, it's wise to not lose that person. Just accept the reality and move on. You will eventually come to terms with it and perhaps laugh at it in future. I don't believe in the theory of *"once a cheater, always a cheater"* when it comes to intense romantic relationships. People can change, and if a person is truly repentant and wants to salvage the relationship, it can be done. I cannot imagine how hard it is, but there are many incredible stories of couples bouncing back from a cheating incident and growing a deeper, stronger love. Infidelity is often a culmination of various relationship problems coming to a head. For couples recovering from infidelity, therapy can be instrumental in helping to tackle all issues in a relationship.

Then there is another type of cheater who will never feel guilty or sorry for cheating. These people who get caught or are guilty of infidelity will casually apologize (without meaning it) and try to convince you that the real fault was of the person they cheated you with!

If your partner doesn't own up to their actions and simply blames it on the other person for *"seducing"* or *"attracting"* them, then there are chances that they will cheat on you again in future because they have given the power to control them to a third person. It is wise to stay away from people who cannot take responsibility of their actions.

"Nobody can influence you unless you want to get influenced. Cheating is a choice."

Many a times, cheaters tend to rationalize their behavior in their own minds. One way they do this is to push the blame onto you. They tell themselves that you don't look the way you used to when they first met you, or you are not seductive enough in the bedroom, or you don't appreciate all the wonderful things they do for you, so they deserve to have a little fun elsewhere.

Often, their internal justifications for cheating leak out and they behave judgmentally towards you and your relationship. Get rid of such people ASAP!

But how to realize that your partner is cheating on you?

Well, there is no perfect answer for it because even if I list out things which cheaters often do, it may happen that your partner also does the same things but is in fact, extremely loyal to you.

Still if you want to examine in detail then carefully observe and check out these things :-

1. Excessive secret use of phone, deleting messages and call history and not telling you with whom they are talking or from whom they are getting frequent texts/calls during personal hours.

2. They spend way too much money these days and cannot give you a reasonable explanation for the same.

3. You have a gut feeling about their infidelity.

4. When your partner suddenly starts dressing too well while leaving the house or meetings.

5. When they regularly vanish without any reason and are not reachable most of the time.

Again a gentle reminder, it may happen that your partner does all these things and yet is not cheating on you. These are just some of the things that people generally do when they are cheating.

But why do people cheat?

There are many reasons for it.

1. One reason is that they are juvenile, naive and nincompoop. These people have simply made a stupid, silly and senseless choice.

2. People cheat because they are not attracted to or excited enough with their partner, or their partner is not giving them enough attention or love. Whatever the reason is, infidelity is wrong and cannot be justified.

3. Some idiots just cheat on their partners to take revenge after an argument or a fight. I mean seriously? How pathetic and shallow!

4. Some people may naturally have needs which cannot be satisfied with just one partner. Despite our idealistic notions of having only one ultimate love, it is possible to experience intense romantic love for multiple people at the same time. While such situations are emotionally possible, they are very complicated and tend to create a lot of anxiety and stress. It is simply their nature to not be *"exclusive"* to one person. They may not have malicious intentions, they may even be happy and satisfied in their relationship but it is just the way they are. Sometimes they are not in control of their urge. They are probably sex addicts or do not believe in monogamy. They cannot fight their natural personality and characteristic. Only get into a relationship with such people if you are comfortable with them sleeping around with a lot of people.

5. Some people are simply untrustworthy. They will be selfish enough to give more importance to their lust over your feelings. They will repeatedly cheat on you at every level be it physical, emotional, financial etc. Get rid of them immediately! Loyalty is an expensive gift; don't expect it from cheap people.

6. Some people cheat because they are out of touch with the reality. They still want the same amount of passion which you had when your relationship began. Their unreasonable expectations and entitlement to constant pleasure and excitement can lead them to infidelity. Sometimes, they perceive that your relationship has become boring, dull or stagnant. They will focus on what is missing in your relationship instead of focusing on what you both already have.

7. Some cheat because they are not satisfied with you. It is a complex situation. It is not completely their fault (though the choice they made is wrong). Your partner does not have the right to cheat on you if you don't give them enough satisfaction.

8. They need to talk and discuss this with you in detail and both of you should work on it together. When it comes to emotional satisfaction, it is more of your fault if you don't spend enough time with your partner, are ignorant, neglect them, take them for granted or not try to understand their feelings. In such cases, the partners will find another shoulder to cry on and hear them out. They will not be attached to you anymore because of your lack of interest in them and their emotions.

9. Many people cheat because they feel sleeping with others will improve their sense of self-worth, signal their independence or increase their social status and popularity. Some may cheat because they want to be a part of a *"group"* or a *"gang"*. I know people who cheat because their group of friends regularly cheat on their partners by visiting brothels or having affairs and they accompany them and do the same just to be accepted as *"one of them"*. Instead of setting a correct example to their friends, they choose to encourage undesirable behavior out of their fear of being different or being mocked.

Loyalty is not as simple and as idealistic as we think it is. There are deep layers to it. If one thinks pragmatically, then it can be concluded that loyalty is a combination of a person's ethics, principles and morals and also of the level of satisfaction and happiness received from their relationship and their partner. There are also people who simply cheat whenever they get an opportunity. There is no pre-determined plan or motivation. They just do it whenever they get a chance.

Regarding infidelity, men are more likely to list motivations having to do with sexual desire, while women confessed that being neglected by their partners lead them to cheat, according to many surveys and studies.

If you have been cheated on, you might be experiencing a whirlwind of emotions. You may feel devastated one moment and angry the next. A broken heart can lead to feelings of shame, doubt, confusion and anxiety.

It is important to not blame yourself for your partner's actions because excessive self-blame can delay the recovery process and make it harder to move on.

Rather than suppressing your emotions, work through them. Accepting the reality is always the first step of the healing process. Also, don't live in the past and replay your entire relationship constantly in your head. Don't ever regret falling in love with the wrong person.

Focus on the present and be grateful for the things you have. Learn from your experiences.

Most people have difficulty concentrating on their studies or at work. Many find it hard to get the energy or desire to take care of themselves but it is necessary to eat and sleep well, share your thoughts and feelings with people, make new friends, focus on your health and career and reconnect to people who genuinely wish well for you, like your parents or friends.

Always remember…

"Your value doesn't decrease based on someone's inability to see your worth."

CHAPTER 7

"HEARTBREAK"

Oh here we are, addressing the Elephant in the room. Welcome to the most unavoidable part of loving someone — the heartbreak. It is one of the greatest suffering that one can go through. The saddest part of life is being separated from someone with whom you wished to spend your entire life. Heartbreak is evidence that you loved someone in good faith. Only the one deeply inside our heart can shatter it. Our brain registers the emotional pain of heartbreak in the same way as physical pain, which is why you might feel like your heartbreak is causing actual physical hurt. It might even be possible to die of a broken heart! People who are in the early stages of grief are more likely to experience increased blood pressure and heart rate, which can raise their cardiovascular risk. People who have their heart broken often suffer from *"Anhedonia"* which is the inability of feel pleasure in normally pleasurable activities and losing interest in enjoying. They just don't feel like caring at all.

People who haven't gone through a heart break are curious, scared or clueless but those who have faced this situation can say that it is quite traumatizing. There is a misconception about heartbreaks that it only occurs after getting separated or breaking up with your lover. Actually in reality if you love someone, heartbreaks are unavoidable part of your day to day life.

You give a person the power to deeply affect you and that person may intentionally or unintentionally do something which can really break your heart.

Heartbreaks can be caused due to smallest of things as well (which don't remain small anymore because the impact of these things is often magnified as compared to the same thing done by a random person whom you don't love). Little things that your partner does like, not complimenting you when you wear your favourite outfit, forgetting your mother's sister's child's birthday, not replying to your text messages immediately, not picking up your calls within 3 seconds, not sending you photos when you ask them to, postponing a date due to emergency etc. can also break your heart, when you are in love. You become "hypersensitive" in love and hence every little thing which doesn't go according to your expectations can break your heart.

We often connect heartbreak with separation. However, heartbreaks are very common and gradually people learn to handle them. In many cases, a heart-break caused due to reasons like arguments and fights can actually build a relationship stronger when the partners patch up, accept each other's flaws and learn to handle adverse situations in a better way.

It is also psychological that if you like somebody and you break their heart; you will always put more efforts to make them happy out of your own guilt.

Everybody goes through a heart-break.

Now let's talk about the bigger issue related to heart-break which is separation or break up.

Please note that this chapter talks about proper hardcore separation and it shouldn't be confused with regular, small *"breakup-patch up fights"* which spans for just a couple of days.

Many times, in spite of trying your best to save a relationship, you fail. It may not be your fault. It may not be anybody's fault. Sometime things are just not meant to happen.

A lot of issues can result into separation. It is very difficult to digest the fact that the amazing bond which you once shared with someone will no longer exist.

We often tend to remember only the happy memories after a breakup but while being in a relationship, we mostly see the issues and the negative side and take the positives for granted.

It is a basic human nature. Sometimes when we are single, we see happy couples and when we are in a relationship, we see happy singles!

So, when you remember the happy memories of your relationship, you not only cherish them but also want to go back to your partner and re-live them. But it is not always possible.

They may have got into another relationship or might have shifted to another place or perhaps have vanished completely out of your life. Many of you would have been blocked by your former lover on all social media platforms as well. It's best to move on and cherish the good times.

There are several reasons for separation and it mostly varies from person to person but the main question is how to deal with heart-break?

Some of you may decide that you will never ever be in a relationship again or think love is not for you or love is pathetic etc. Some will lose faith in trust, loyalty or even goodness of humanity. Some will lose hope for a good partner. Some will get bitter and stop trusting people and responding to love they receive from others. That is certainly not the right way to deal with it. Another common tendency which I notice among the youth to deal with a broken heart is to quickly get into another relationship as soon as possible or have flings and superficial rebound. This is not a wise thing to do because it will only make you feel sexy or worthwhile, temporarily. Once that high wears off, you may just feel nothing but guilt, hurt, emptiness or regret.

Romantic movies and sitcoms have taught us that it is easy to get over a heart break and move on. We have been shown since many years that all we have to do is watch sad movies in our pajamas, sob into a bowl of ice cream for two days straight, listen to sad songs, get drunk, party with our friends, bump into someone attractive and we have successfully moved on.

These things are all easier said than done. In reality, you may find yourself picking up some terrible habits like ignoring your friends, neglecting your studies/work and generally not practicing any self-care. You will not be able to sleep well at night if you are not at peace with your heart-break. You will simply try to show others that you are happy but deep inside you will continue to be sad and have a lot of frustration and angst.

This suppressed anger will be taken out on other people who have no idea what's going inside your mind. So, the best way is to stop pretending to be happy, accept the situation, be at peace and honestly talk to someone who can understand your feelings and thoughts. You may talk to your best friend, parents, relatives, boss, pet or even simply to the wall. When you speak things and let it out from your system, you release all the negativity, angst, frustration, anger and sadness out of your body which in a way helps in cleansing your mind, body and soul. Lift yourself up emotionally, mentally, and physically. Allow yourself to cry. Don't suppress your stress and emotions as it will only cause you depression and pain. There is no need to be embarrassed or ashamed of your heartbreak. The painful situations that caused it were real and legitimate and so are the emotions you are battling with. Cry your heart out. Cry for hours, days or weeks till your heart is satisfied. But once you stop crying, never look back again. The process of self- healing is nothing but discomfort – acceptance – growth. If necessary, take medical help of doctors, certified counselors or therapists. Find happiness within yourself.

If you always think that your happiness is in someone else or somewhere else, it will never be where you are. A more mature way of handling pain is self-introspection. It will give you a correct perspective. It is also important to have empathy and think from your former lover's point of view.

Try to find out what went wrong, evaluate what you gained from the relationship and what you gave up for it, the lessons you learnt from this experience and what were the reasons and circumstances which lead to any one of you making the choice of splitting up.

If you think holistically, try to understand the larger picture and leave aside your small world for a second, then you will realize that what happened is best for you and also for your former partner, in most cases. Never indulge in taking any kind of "revenge" or put efforts in making your ex-partner feel that they lost someone really special. Don't start posting unnecessary pictures of your perfect body post work out, or you wearing a sexy attire to attract your partner and make them regret their decision, or make them jealous by acting overly friendly with someone more attractive or richer than them.

It is an absolute waste of time and energy. Accept peacefully that they broke your heart, they don't want you anymore or your relationship didn't work out and move on. Don't try to *"win them back"* or put bitter/sad/revengeful posts in your social media stories or status for them to see, the one who broke your heart doesn't care. If someone doesn't want to be with you then why to manipulate them into being with you just to satisfy your ego or for your sense of achievement in "getting them back"?

Have some dignity and self-respect. Influencing someone to be with you against their natural desire is not a good approach for the long term because that manipulation will eventually wear off and they will soon regret their decision to be with you again and would want to distance themselves from you and you will end up wasting your time and energy and will again get your heart broken. Sometimes, not getting what you want can be the most precious and enlightening experience of your life.

At the end of the day, if your intentions are pure, you will be blessed for sure.

Don't always expect a perfect closure. Unfortunately, what tends to happen is that two people slowly drift apart, and after the split, one of you is left wondering, why?

One thing you need to understand is that underneath the desperate need for closure is a desire to get back together. Sometimes, it is important to not unnecessarily drag things if your relationship isn't working out. I don't encourage impulsive break-ups but at times one should not try to fix things which are meant to be broken. End things on a happy note. Don't indulge in blame game – *"You left me when I needed you the most.", "Why did you let me go, you could have stopped me.", "You broke my heart in spite of everything I did for you."* are some of the things people normally say to each other when they are heart broken.

Stop judging who was right and who was wrong. Have good memories of the wonderful times you both spent together and cherish your treasured memories. Sometimes people can be in your heart but not in your life. Accept it and move on. Don't get bitter and lose hope. Learn from the mistakes and experiences.

Someone much better is out there waiting for you and when you meet that person, you will automatically understand that why things didn't work out with anyone else. Bad relationships help you to understand the value and importance of a good relationship.

However, before you meet that someone special who was always meant to be *"the one"*, you will have to learn to deal with loneliness. It is extremely important to learn to enjoy your own company.

> *"You don't need anyone to make you happy, happiness comes from within."*

Yes, I know that you are broken but broken crayons colour the same as new crayons. Do things which you couldn't do while in a relationship, catch up with your old friends, spend time with family, exercise, help others, do social work, follow your passion and pursue your hobbies, spend time with yourself, focus on your career etc. Talk to people, sometimes you think that you don't want to interact with anyone and just want to disappear but all you really want is to be found and understood.

There will also be times when you will miss your former partner. It is a very crucial stage of your life and what choices you make now will define your future.

You will have an irresistible urge to talk to them or meet them. There will be a conflict between your mind and heart. You will give excuses to yourself and try your best to convince yourself that you should interact with your ex. You will have thoughts which will provoke you to get back to them like, *"We both can still be friends."*, *"We will only talk occasionally."*, *"He/she knows me so well and understands me like nobody can."*, *"We have spent so much time together and have such wonderful memories."*, *"We were so good together."*, *"Let's give each other one more chance."* etc.

I am personally not a fan of being very close friends with an ex-lover, it can affect your life in various ways which even you cannot predict. Some may misuse the influence they have on you and exploit you for their needs. The one who broke you cannot be the one who will repair and fix you. However, some ex-lovers may be good human beings who would stand by you as "friends" but then again those feelings will come back and only complicate your life further. It is better to simply move on and find other distractions.

The decision is ultimately (and will always be) in your own hands. The temptation is just way too much and it is understandable if you want to talk to them as "just friends" or even try to give another chance to your relationship. But first, learn to deal with your heart break.

"Heart-breaks are important. It gives you a lot of lessons and enables you to grow quickly."

Getting your heart broken can give you a much needed reality check and makes you more pragmatic, mature and realistic. You learn to deal with pain and how to recover from it. The fantasy world that you create in your mind at the initial naive stage of your life comes down crashing and you have to face the hardcore reality of life. You also get to know how human mind functions and to what extent a person can go. You also come to know who your real well wishers are and who are the fake ones. It makes you wiser, calmer, more sorted and patient. It increases your level of understanding of human beings and relationships. It also helps you in keeping your expectations more realistic. You also get to learn a lot about yourself and know your range of emotions and how you react to various circumstances. It will make you strong and independent in many ways.

"Heart-break is an experience which everyone must have at least once in their lives, the sooner the better."

How do you mend a broken heart?

When your entire world is falling apart!

But after all the sufferings,

There will be a moment when you realize,

Even with all the gloom,

You are always free to bloom.

CHAPTER 8

"LOVE HACKS"

Ah, so you want to know some hacks to improve your love life? Well, to be honest there is no shortcut to anything good in life. Even if you manage to get what you want by using short cuts, it won't last long. Anything worthwhile always takes a lot of effort and time. However, you can certainly work in a smarter way. Smart work and hard work both have a very thin line of difference. Both require efforts unlike shortcuts. However, smart work is when a person puts efforts in the right direction with planning and prioritization of tasks which enables him to optimally utilize his time and put correct amount of energy in the most effective, efficient and productive manner. Using the smart way requires more focus than simply working hard for long hours like a Donkey. Smart work means receiving more output than your input. Apply efforts in the right direction at the right time and you will be rewarded abundantly, beyond your expectations.

Like I said in the previous chapters, there is no standard formula to have a perfect relationship. Actually, a perfect relationship is a myth.

Every relationship goes through their ups and downs. It is a roller coaster ride and you have to find your own unique way to make your relationship special. After finding the right person by applying the *"love tests"* as per the first chapter, using the secret recipe for a long lasting relationship according to chapter three and avoiding common conflicts mentioned in the fifth chapter, you are pretty much sorted.

This chapter will give you a unique perspective and help you in putting efforts in the right direction in order to ameliorate your love life.

I won't be giving you hacks like *"indulge in role plays"*, *"learn new things together"*, *"send flowery text messages everyday"*, *"give each other massages"* and similar cheesy stuff. We are here to talk about reality and not delusory fanciful tricks. Honestly, I also cannot give you a list of *"to do things"* and claim that it will work. Different ways work for different individuals, the quicker you learn this, the better it will be for you otherwise you will keep wasting your time in googling things like *"how to do this…"* and *"how to do that…"* and try to apply it in your life thereby failing miserably. However, I can surely give some advice to help you identify your own answers along with a list of things that one should avoid in order to have a blissfully sorted relationship. We normally tend to disrupt our own relationships because of our behaviour. Sometimes not doing anything wrong is the only way to get things right.

So friends, the first thing that any couple should never ever do is **comparison**.

Don't get into any kind of comparisons between your relationship and other relationships and also between your partner and you (who does what, who puts more efforts, who sacrifices more, who apologizes first etc.) because it is a tried and tested way to ruin a relationship.

"Any kind of excessive comparison is a recipe for disaster."

Most people think that if a comparison is given to a person, they will get motivated to better themselves. Not true! It's one of the biggest turn-offs. Never say things like *"He/she looks/cooks/drives/earns so much better than you.", "He gave his partner an expensive diamond.", "Why don't you dress like her?"* or *"You should learn something from him/her."*

Moreover, don't compare your relationship with other couples. Not even with your best friend's or parent's relationship. Every couple has their own journey and their own issues.

Nobody is living a perfect life, irrespective of the fact that how happy they look on social media or how they give out a perfect *"couple goals"* vibe in-person. So, if your best friend's boyfriend/husband takes her on a holiday or buys her an expensive gift, don't expect the same from your guy.

Also, worse, don't compare and express the same to him, he will not be encouraged to do the same for you but on the contrary he will feel disappointed, guilty or demotivated.

Similarly, if your best friend's wife has amazing friendly parents, has a beautiful hairstyle, a wonderful dressing sense, cooks perfectly or has a fabulous job, don't point out to your girl the fact that she doesn't have those privileges.

Similarly, never compare the amount of efforts you both are putting in the relationship. It can lead to a lot of arguments and it's a never ending debate on who is doing more in a relationship. If you start arguing then it will lead to your partner making you count smallest of things they do or have previously done for you which you won't like.

> *"When anyone constantly lists out things they did for you or are doing for you, those things lose their significance and you start feeling less special."*

Eventually you end up listing things that you have sacrificed for the relationship which your partner will also not value and will simply dismiss it in some way or the other, just for the sake of the on-going argument. Yes, if you are in a relationship where there is only one-sided effort from you, then you need to take a call whether you want it or not. If your partner's efforts are negligible, then it is necessary to show the mirror and give them a reality check. One should not be with people who exploit you or takes undue advantage of you. However, if you are in a balanced relationship where sometimes your partner contributes more and sometimes you do, then it is best to be grateful for the smallest of things your partner does for you and never compare your efforts with your partner.

Never get into silly arguments like, *"I always text/call first or text/call more than you do"*, *"I always travel more for our meetings"*, *"I do so much for you and you don't do anything for me"*, *"Your parents-my parents debates"*, *"Your contribution- my contribution arguments"*. It takes two hands to clap and efforts of two people to make any relationship work. There can never be a completely equal relationship, sometimes when your partner is low and down, you need to stand by them and vice versa. The effort ratio can never be exact 50:50. Sometimes it's 70:30, sometimes it can be 20:80 etc.

Having said this, make sure you keep observing and ensuring that you do not blindly put one sided efforts. The ratio of efforts should be balanced in the long run (when your contribution ratio is low, then your partner's should be high) and should be observed holistically.

Another thing which one should never do is take **impulsive decisions**.

I understand that it is not always realistic to expect that individuals should always keep their emotions in control. Nobody can. We feel angry, jealous, sad etc. and these emotions impact our relationships. Also, when two people are involved, chances of making these impulsive decisions due to lack of control over emotions gets doubled.

If you are in a steady relationship and believe that you have found the right person for you, then don't ruin the relationship because of impulsive decisions. Be patient. Think again before taking any final call.

Evaluate the situation and think whether the issue is worth taking such drastic decision or not. Remember the good times you have shared with your partner and the dreams which you both have seen together for your future. A moment of patience in a moment of anger saves a thousand moments of regret.

Human beings are full of flaws and imperfections. You have accepted the person with all their weaknesses, flaws, imperfections, attitude etc. Don't end things or stretch a fight unnecessarily if your partner has knowingly or unknowingly made a mistake.

The impact of any mistake is different for each individual. For someone infidelity may be a small mistake and they forgive their partners, for some even a small abusive word can be a deal breaker. *For example-* I feel that violence (done by either of the partner irrespective of their gender) is a deal breaker but I know a lot of people who get into verbal and physical fights every day and yet have an intense love and companionship. For them hitting each other during a fight is an absolutely normal part of their relationship.

Therefore, mistakes are subjective and their importance varies from person to person. However, the gist of this is to have patience to deal with small irrelevant mistakes and issues caused by your partner.

Don't fulminate and rant about minor blunders of your partner. Forget and forgive. Don't ruin the peace in your relationship. Simply express your disappointment in a very polite and gentle manner.

They will realize how their actions can affect you adversely and if they genuinely care about you, they will mend their ways on their own.

When we are in a relationship, either it is a mutual attraction or one person has made the other person fall in love with him/her. Normally when one person persuades the other to be in a relationship and when the other person reciprocates, it usually happens that the person who made the first move slowly starts taking their partner for granted.

"For some people, getting a person is like winning a trophy."

You must have observed that there are people who put a lot of efforts and keep trying to convince until they get what they want. Then gradually their behaviour changes and they get colder with each passing day. It's like they lose interest once their ego is satisfied after *"getting you"*. Such people feel a sense of accomplishment because they are able to influence a person to get what they want. They have no interest in developing and nurturing a relationship and growing together. Avoid such people.

It is important not to take your partner for granted and always appreciate the smallest of things they do for you. Moreover, avoid being a *"trophy girlfriend"* or a *"trophy boyfriend"* for anyone. When a person dates you under the pretense that they love you but actually they are just dating you for your good looks and to keep flaunting you in front of their friends and public, then my dear, you are in a trophy relationship.

The reason your partner keeps you around is, so they can use you for an ego boost, to prove to the world that there is nothing wrong with them, to prove that they are lovable, or they believe it will increase their popularity amongst their peers and public, and they feel flaunting you around as a prized possession is considered as a status symbol. This behaviour from your partner can make you feel like an object with no individuality.

Another crucial advice I would like to give is to **be realistic**. It is unreasonable for me to ask you to never expect anything from your partner.

How can you love someone, give your everything to the relationship and never expect anything in return? It is impossible and unnatural. However, in order to prevent getting hurt and disappointed it is better to keep your expectations reasonable. Don't burden your partner or your relationship with unrealistic expectations.

For example – Your expectations are unrealistic and unreasonable if you expect your partner to do the following :-

1. Give up their friends and hobbies for you,

2. "Always" having perfectly pleasurable and satisfying time irrespective of their mood,

3. Leave all their work aside and always be available for you whenever you call them even for the smallest of things,

4. Keep the house spotlessly clean all the time like your mother did,

5. Look like Chris Hemsworth/Scarlet Johansson or whosoever gets you going,

6. To anticipate your every need without you even communicating,

7. You expect your partner to pay for (basically) everything,

8. You expect your partner to spend all their free time with you.

Keep things real. Be aware of your partner's financial, physical, romantic, social or emotional capacity. It is important to keep evolving but don't push them so much that your relationship gets ruined. Also, introspect often and know what exactly are you expecting and how reasonable it is. If you don't know what your expectations are, your partner will have a hard time reaching them because you might always be moving the goal post. You surely don't want to come across as confused, greedy, ungrateful or too demanding. When two people are able to compromise and come together with matched expectations, nothing short of magic happens.

Moreover, even when you are contributing something in your relationship and doing something special for your partner to make them happy, make sure you give them "what they want" and not "what you want to give". You don't get to decide what should make them happy.

If your objective is to make them feel special, you have to observe them (or simply ask them) and understand what gives them joy.

Don't assume randomly or generalize things based on stereotypes. Don't give what is convenient to you. If your partner is sensible, they will politely accept your gift and be grateful but they will never actually feel the joy from within.

One more thing which you should avoid is getting into a relationship for the sake of it.

This is very common among today's youth. Everybody wants to date for various reasons. Some want to have physical intimacy, some want emotional support, some need financial assistance, some want a companion to accompany them everywhere, some want a partner to show off on social media and some get into a relationship because it is in fashion and everybody is doing it.

Relationship is not a pastime; it is a full time job. If you cannot handle it don't apply for it. It is an experience which will shape your personality and your future.

Before the Victorian era, relationships were business based, often set up by parents in an attempt to form allegiances farms or countries. There was no pressure to *"love forever"* or be your partner's best friend and fidelity was rarely even discussed. The idea of a relationship has evolved with time into something that is supposed to define us and be the focal point of our lives. Go ahead wisely.

Another common mistake that I often see these days is people **text a lot** instead of calling or meeting.

I completely understand that many of you have time constraints and one can multi-task while texting their partners which enables them to balance their love life with other important things. Also, it is a quick way to communicate multiple things at once. However, what I want to emphasize here is that texting is good but only up to a point. When important things are to be discussed, have a telephonic conversation or the best way is to simply meet.

It is not wise to debate over texts because a person may read and interpret text messages according to their own mood. Imagine, if someone is angry and you text them something which further annoys them, then you will have to face their ferocity. Text messages can easily be misunderstood since the tone of the person cannot be comprehended accurately.

So, it is highly recommended that you have only basic small talks and sharing of information over text messages to save time and to constantly "be in touch", but never indulge in serious discussions over text messages. I have seen people breaking up over text messages and directly blocking their partner's numbers, something which could have been avoided if they had discussed in-person.

One of the fascinating things which I have minutely observed everywhere from rural areas to metro cities, is the way couples **deal with anger** and how it can often make or break a relationship. Anger is a basic human emotion. Everybody gets angry. It is normal but how you react, is what really matters.

Whenever you are furious at you partner, don't settle for screaming, abusing, violence, breaking things and slamming doors. Anger needs to be managed well in order to avoid serious consequences. Moreover, anger can also be contagious and both people in the relationship often end up angry. It is important to not look at arguments as *"You vs them"* but look as *"You both vs the issue"*. Managing anger and managing your response to an angry partner is a useful skill that can promote intimacy and maturity in any romantic relationship.

I personally recommend your partner and you to mutually decide and make an unbreakable rule to have one *"cool down word"* (it can be anything, even something absurd) which if any of you speak in the middle of a fight, the other person HAS TO simply stop the fight right there and stay calm. Trust me, it works. Whenever you think a fight is going out of control and can result into something serious, just say that word and cool down. You both need to have a word which will automatically stop the fight, however big it is. *For example* – I know a couple whose cool down word is *"Pikachu"* because both of them were fond of Pokémon in their childhood.

One day, they got into a fight and in the heat of the moment were about to hit each other when suddenly the girl said *"Pikachu"* and the guy stopped.

The guy also said *"Pikachu"* and the girl also cooled down. Both of them stayed silent for a while, then hugged each other and patched up.

That's the power of the cool down word. It will give you time to calm down, rethink and resolve your argument. Be carefully not to overuse this word, otherwise it will lose its importance and won't work. Use it only when there is an emergency and you feel that the fight or an argument is going beyond control and will cause tremendous harm to your relationship.

When someone is really pissed (because of you or some other reason) and they ask you to leave them alone for a while then trust me, **STAY AWAY**. I know you care for them and want to uplift their mood but they don't need your help at the moment, they just want to be alone. If there is a fight between you both and they ask you to give them some lone time, don't argue because at that point of time they are at a saturation point where they will simply avoid all arguments and just end things right there, even if the issue is really small and irrelevant. Trying to coerce or threatening them into a quick reconciliation after a fight or pressurizing them to share their thoughts is likely to backfire and cause them to cutoff even more. Give them a reasonable cooling period instead of being clingy or arguing beyond their mental capacity.

One more love hack which is really important and can improve your love life - **Respect each other's timing**. Some sleep early, some sleep late, some have different working hours, some study/work extra hard, some travel far, some have a lot of family responsibilities etc. It is necessary to respect each other's timing.

If your partner comes home late and is tired due to working hard the entire day, don't make them watch your favourite show or movie, or ask them to describe their day in detail, keep giving them gossips or make them play videogames with you. And please use head phones while watching something when they are asleep or relaxing. Trust me, they are in no mood to listen to anything, they simply want to relax and sleep well.

It is important to give space to your partner. Having said this, it is equally important to spend quality time with your partner. Both partners should blend their timings and schedules and make sure they at least talk to each other every day, share their emotions, watch movies or take road trips on weekends and have at least one meal together. People who are in a long distance relationship can identify some mutual interests which you and your partner have and through the power of modern technology (Skype, Facetime, WhatsApp) connect with each other.

It could be as simple as having a *"virtual dinner"* together on Skype or Zoom where you talk about each other's day or as interactive as a live dance-off where you both select songs and dance, or as soothing as singing songs for each other.

One of the most important things to completely enjoy your relationship is to **be in the moment**.

Love with abandon and don't be afraid of the uncertain future. Don't ruin your present while worrying about the future, yet be observant and aware of your dynamics with your partner.

During your dating phase, try to know each other better instead of trying to "possess" that person and ruining things by being insecure and expecting too much from the future and ultimately getting disappointed. Yes, when we decide to be with someone it is natural to think about the future but in planning and anticipating future we often miss out the joy of living in the present. Cherish each and every moment with your partner. Don't try to hold a particular moment and get anxious whether things will work out in future or not. It will be a foolish thing to do if instead of enjoying the moment, you keep worrying whether your partner will continue to love you and whether your relationship will stay the same or will it deteriorate. Just let it be. Relish the blissful moments and continue to make memories. Go with the flow.

Life unfolds in the present. But so often, we let the present slip away, allowing time to rush past unobserved and unseized and squandering the precious seconds of our lives as we worry about the future and ruminate about the past. Most of us don't undertake our thoughts in awareness. Rather, our thoughts control us. We need to live more in the moment.

It will ultimately make you happier, more exuberant, more empathetic and more secure with higher self-esteem which in a way will help you to contribute positively to your relationship instead of being cynical or anxious.

As I mentioned in the third chapter, honesty is extremely important to have a long lasting relationship. But let me tell you something more beneficial, you can do better than simply not lying.

All you have to do is never keep secrets from your partner. The best relationships are when people can be lovers and best friends at the same time and are completely open and honest with each other. One shouldn't be afraid to share parts of themselves with their partner. A strong sense of safety and trust is necessary for sharing secrets with each other – secrets that reveal your greatest interests, desires, dreams and disappointments. Sharing secrets increases intimacy, builds trust and strengthens your bond. Honour each other by being a safe place for your partner to share their secrets.

When you first get into a relationship, it is totally natural to feel like you want to spend a lot of time together. You often live in your own little fantasy bubble and that is a really amazing and intoxicating place to be. While you may think that the ultimate goal of a relationship is to spend 24 hours a day with your partner, never getting bored of each other or wanting to do anything apart, but in reality, the most productive and loving relationships involve a decent amount of alone time. Always keep a little space and *"me time"* to improve your relationship.

Space in a relationship doesn't affect your happy moment together. It benefits both individuals involved in the relationship, as it prevents the bond from falling apart. A lot of people complain that they have lost their identity in their relationship because they don't know who they are without their partner, and that is why space is important. Couples need space, so they don't suffocate each other. Having time apart encourages independence and freshness in a relationship.

You will be happier and your relationship will bloom. In a relationship, spending time alone helps you to appreciate your partner and reminds you how much you both love each other.

"Me time" can allow you to reconnect with what is important to you and can be used to enhance the connection you have with your partner. For people who are just starting out and are figuring whether a person can be a potential partner or whether you actually love them or not — try to not meet them every day.

"If you daily meet someone, attachment is bound to happen but if you don't meet them regularly and you still feel attached then my dear, you are in love."

It brings memories of exciting moments and strengthens the mutual feelings towards each other. To explain you the importance of distance and space let me give you a psychological hypothesis. Ever heard of the *Westermarck Effect?*

Well, the Westermarck Effect is basically what keeps us from being sexually attracted to our siblings. It hypothesizes that people who live *"in close domestic proximity"* during the first few years of life will become desensitized to sexual attraction to each other. While you and your partner aren't children, there have been studies that suggest that even adults living together develop a familiar feelings towards each other that can kill sexual attraction. Less time together is a good way to counteract those feelings. A bit of space and distance is necessary in your relationship. Trust me, you will excitedly look forward to spending more time with your partner.

Absence really does make the heart grow fonder. The best way to appreciate something or someone is to be without them for a while.

Another love hack to have a wonderful relationship is to have **empathy.** Your relationship can go for a toss when you assume that your partner has the same needs and boundaries as you do and that they experience life the same way as well. A relationship without empathy quickly hits a bump. The goal of empathy in a relationship is to understand and feel as closely as possible what is going on in your partner's mind and heart. This is a skill that you can learn, not an inherent trait that you are born with. You develop empathy within a relationship by regularly listening to each other's thoughts and feelings.

Seeing the world from your partner's perspective helps to build closeness as well as respect for your partner's individuality. Also, when your partner is letting their emotions out and showing you their vulnerable side, don't judge them, try to suppress their emotions, ignore them or downplay their venting by calling it *"overreaction"*. It is also advisable to never give them advice when they are venting, unless they ask you for it. Unsolicited advice will make them feel frustrated and unsupported. Empathize with them instead and be interested in knowing their thoughts and if required, validate them through supportive feedback.

Finally, one of the most important hacks to have a blissfully sorted relationship is to have **financial equality**.

Financial conflict is highly nuanced and manifests differently in every relationship. It is also heavily influenced by social and cultural expectations as well as personal values. These expectations, combined with money and relationships, can surface feelings like inadequacy, unworthiness and discontent, leading to stress and mental health problems like guilt (for partners who earn less), concealing spending habits and financial power struggle.

A partner who earns more, often wants to make important decisions. Observe your current financial relationship dynamics carefully. It is important to let both partners feel in control of their financial situations. There is no single best way to split expenses in a relationship, unfortunately. Every relationship and each person's financial circumstances are different. *For example*, you and your partner may agree that splitting household expenses 50-50 may be tough for the lower earner in the relationship, but paying for a dinner date is manageable for the partner who earns less.

Equality doesn't mean everything should be rigidly equal. It means that the person who brings less income should be contributing a higher value in another area of the relationship than the high-salary earner.

Money plays an important role, and as it turns out, people are 10 times more likely to break up if they think their partner is bad with their finances.

People are raised to think about saving, spending, and investing differently.

Therefore, in the process of knowing each other before or during your relationship, make sure you know about your partner's financial habits.

Just like a movie date or a dinner date, plan a *"financial date"* where you both discuss each other's finances, investments, goals, debts, spending habits etc. Having a financial equality keeps both the partners invested and promotes trust, transparency, commitment and teamwork.

So friends, these were some of the hacks to improve your love life. I am sure they will be extremely useful. Just make sure you hit the bull's eye when it comes to choosing your partner. Forget all the "cheesy romantic things" that you have watched, heard of or read about because they are far from the reality. It is not needed that your partner or potential partner always "completes your sentences" or immediately knows what you are thinking or magically appears whenever you think about them, if they give their 100% to your relationship and do all they can for you, that's good enough.

CHAPTER 9

"LETTERS OF WISDOM"

Here we are, on the second last chapter of this book. As a farewell bonus, I have written personalized letters for females and males respectively. Calling my own letters "Letters of Wisdom" might sound a bit pompous, eh? I know. But in my defense, the content of these letters are compiled from life experiences of a lot of people across different age groups, with different perspectives and unique personalities, with whom I had the opportunity to interact on various occasions. I am merely rephrasing and simplifying it for you. It will help you introspect your lives and also inspire you to make the best of it. So, let's begin…ladies first.

Dear girls,

Hope you are doing well in life and this book helps you in learning more about love and relationships. I know that the world hasn't been particularly fair with females since centuries. Most of you have faced constant abuses, discrimination, disparity, exploitations and inequality in some way or the other.

A lot of females have fought for their basic rights and continue to fight for equality but still at the core our patriarchal society is intentionally or unintentionally, very male chauvinistic and unfair. I personally believe that female is the stronger gender and they normally have to go through a lot as compared to men. Women generally have a stronger emotional quotient than men; they get mature quickly and are more giving. For example, a 14 year old girl is much more mature and emotionally stable compared to a 14 year old boy.

Many men complain that why do intellectuals always consider females stronger than men?

I think they will never understand what all a female has to go through in her entire life. One small example of 'male versus female' comparison regarding physical and mental strength would be that if men started having periods, bleed excessively, have cravings & mood swings and feel the pain of menstrual cramps, then they wouldn't be able to handle it, or would get insane and perhaps would be running on the roads stabbing people like maniacs!

Many people say that giving birth to a new life is the most beautiful feeling ever but it's also the most painful feeling. It is believed that while giving birth, the pain caused to a woman is equivalent to the pain of breaking all bones of her body! Only women can go through this level of pain. Giving birth is considered to be a second life for a lady in popular culture. Apart from this, the amount of multi-tasking which females do is beyond imagination of any man.

Therefore, women are emotionally & mentally stronger, have a higher threshold for pain and their survival and management skills are superior to their male counterpart, in most cases. However, even this characteristic is often misused by people. Since her childhood, a girl is taught to sacrifice and compromise, be it for her brother, then for her husband and then for her children. Even in our fairytales, a girl is always psychologically an annex of a father, a "prince" or other male figure. Traditionally, in films also, mostly the "hero" shows his heroism by saving the "girl" from the villains.

If a person has limited amount of money and has an option to either educate his son or his daughter, most people will educate their son even if their daughter is more competent and intelligent. A preference for sending boys to school is fuelled by a belief that all girls will eventually get married off.

A celebration of an achievement is also different for males and females — when a boy achieves something; it is hugely celebrated while an achievement of a girl is not given as much importance. It is not that the family doesn't love their daughters (unfortunately some orthodox people still don't) but unintentionally people bring up their children very differently. A boy is given a lot of privileges and a girl is taught to do household work.

If you notice in your house as well, irrespective of the fact that how educated you are or how much money you earn, your parents will force you to learn cooking, even if it doesn't interest you. A girl is always expected to cook and learn to "take care of the house".

*I have actually noticed many families where the boy comes home from school and throws away his bag, his shoes, his socks and his uniform in the living room and his sister is asked by the parents to collect those things and keep them in the right place. The girl does it happily for her family but they don't raise her the way she should be raised — with equality. A girl has to face discrimination in the education system, even during her exams she has to study and also help her mother in the kitchen or in household work, it gets even worse when she is in her periods or is not healthy and yet she is expected to endure the pain and continue to do her "duties". A teenage or a young adult male child is given complete freedom to hang out with his friends, even come home late at night or sometimes have a night stay but the girl has to ask for permissions, convince her parents, and in spite of all the efforts of getting permission to go out, gets a deadline before which she has to return home. English makes it a challenge too, which terms you as "wo-**man**," and "fe-**male**," indirectly calling you a "variation" and not worthy in our own right of a title.*

You must have observed that in all the family functions or events, the most common question thrown at you will be "when are you getting married?"

You might be highly educated, have a successful career, be financially independent and have the best possible life but yet most people only want to know when are you getting "settled"?

Many girls are taught that they are a "gift to men" and their final objective in life is to marry and settle down with a good guy. Gender inequality continues to grant men and boys with more rights, privileges and opportunities to become key decision makers and influencers.

Girls and women, however, are denied opportunities to develop themselves and improve their social conditions – simply because they are female.

Women have been relegated to the domestic sphere, while gender roles have depicted men as more fit for public life, leadership positions, and activities in business and politics. Even while writing this, I cannot imagine what all things you go through on daily basis, perhaps things which I have listed is just a small part of it. Many scoundrels don't even allow a girl child to take birth. Their logic is that a boy is an asset, will carry their legacy forward and will take care of his parents when they get old while a girl child is considered a liability because a lot of expenses will be incurred on her marriage and once married she will be shifted to her new home. I mean how stupid! What I have personally observed these days is that most women take better care of their parents even after their marriage while some men make their parents feel unwanted or often throw their old parents in old age homes on slightest of disputes. That's karma.

A lady is the creator of life, she gives birth (another thing which men will never been able to understand and empathize with — the journey of those 9 months of pregnancy).

Most girls I meet have faced a lot of inequality which has led them to question their own worth. Since childhood, girls have been thrust upon added pressure to be "perfect". An overweight girl is body shamed while a fat guy is called healthy.

A guy with many girlfriends is called a "stud" while a girl with many boyfriends is called a "slut". Boys get away with bad behaviour and abusing whereas girls are always expected to be polite and well-mannered. People get shocked when a girl smokes or drinks but the same people very casually accept when a boy does the same. There is also always a huge pay gap between males and females. Often, females are paid much less at workplace compared to men with same qualification and experience, for doing the same work. Also, females are more likely expected to take career breaks and they hold fewer executive and top positions in most organizations. Unfortunately, the list of inequality is endless.

Even when we talk about romantic relationships, girls often have a higher risk of getting into toxic relationships. Confused? Well, let me explain and simplify it for you.

As a girl you might have noticed that you always get a lot of attention from the opposite gender as compared to generally what guys get from girls. Be it social media requests/text messages/proposals etc. You will always have a lot of choice, and that is also quite dangerous because you will have to act responsibly, choose the best out of many. There is a very high probability to choose the wrong one.

However, no pressure, even if you choose the wrong guy, it will be a lesson and that bitter experience will help you appreciate the right guy more and will also enable you to grow as person. I can imagine that irrespective of your age, colour, size, height and overall looks, you all get a lot of messages from random strangers who want to interact with you, you get a lot of likes, comments and compliments on your photos as compared to what a guy of your parallel gets. If you don't like someone, just politely deny them. If they try to cross the line, then be firm and don't tolerate any kind of harassment.

I know many girls who don't take a firm stand for themselves when a guy crosses line. Sometimes they are intimidated, sometimes they don't want to come across as "rude" (yes, few girls have actually given me this reason for their tolerance to harassment from guys). Some girls don't want to spoil their friendly equation with a friend who occasionally flirts with them.

Many girls have irrationally accepted the stereotypes and say things like "men will be men" and "if a boy teases you, it means he likes you" and tolerate obscene or crude behaviour. These lines gives out a wrong narrative and many guys think that it is okay to use coercive methods to pursue a girl. Trust me, you are doing nothing but encouraging those guys to cross line more frequently.

DO NOT normalize indecency.

It is not okay if someone says something inappropriate (even if he is your friend).

Take a stand for your dignity and deal firmly with the wrong guys. Now let's talk about the right guys. Too rare these days, eh?

Since you get a lot of attention from so many guys, it is very important to choose the right guy out of so many options. To be absolutely realistic, nobody knows the future, it all depends on your destiny as well as how you handle different situations and take the right decisions.

However, I can suggest you that go for the guy that makes you happy, the one who has honesty, respectfulness and loyalty as prime characteristics. The one who treats you like an equal and unlocks that cage put around you by the society and hands you your own keys. Don't be swayed by "coolness quotient", popularity, money or good looks because all that is temporary and these are certainly not the right criteria to select a partner.

The toxic guys are mostly very charming, rich, attractive and they often say the "right things" (which you want to hear or like to hear) while the "good guys" are often very simplistic, may not be very rich or good at speaking flirty lines or sending charming messages, may not bring you gifts and flowers or pull your chair or open doors for you etc. but you need to see their intention and willingness to love and support you every single day of your life. I have observed many girls and their families losing their sense of objectivity and going crazy when they come across a potential partner who is either an NRI or a Green card holder or is bloody wealthy. This is certain not the best criteria to select a partner and this greed of wealth has often destroyed lives of many girls.

Also, I see a lot of girls who miss out on good guys because of the misconceptions in their own minds. Many girls want a guy to make "efforts" in proposing them. But their definition of effort is often unrealistic. I know girls who" play hard to get" just to ensure that the guy puts more efforts. I don't think it is a wise thing to do if you actually like the guy because most nice guys believe in "consent" and will immediately back off if you don't give them an encouraging response.

Good guys will never "chase you" or pursue you, they are often very straightforward and will respect and accept your decision. So, if you like a guy and he approaches you, and you play hard to get, he won't come back again. And then if you say he didn't "put enough effort", then you are wrong and you have just lost a gem who believes in consent, respects your decision and is a dignified self-respecting guy.

Let's assume you are in a relationship with a wonderful guy, still you will continue to get attention from many guys, even if they know that you are committed.

Make sure you avoid such unwanted attention and don't indulge in unnecessary, over-friendly conversations which can lead to problems in your current relationship. Even when you have fights with your partner, don't start responding to those hungry dogs as "a punishment" to your partner. Moreover, don't respond to such fuck boys in order to be "polite".

If you don't respond to their texts, deny their proposals on their face or ignore their unwanted attention, it is completely okay. Don't get pressurized to positively respond to them even out of courtesy. You don't need to.

Be realistic, these guys who keep showering compliments to you are not doing it because they find you special, such people do it to every other girl they meet in person or interact online. You are simply one of those hundreds of girls they flirt with so don't take them too seriously.

They just want to show off their flirting skills, or they need to win some bet for successfully wooing you or they want some kind of revenge from you or your partner or they simply want to get laid. Don't compare and say that your partner doesn't compliment you or doesn't make you feel special while this random guy online or at your college, workplace or neighborhood is giving you so much attention. Try to understand the intentions of people.

Never get affected by peer pressure. I know a lot of girls who are very "simple" and yet just to "fit in" they drink, smoke, wear skimpy clothes, get into affairs and try to be wild just so that they can present themselves as "modern", independent, strong and open minded girls. This is actually a very stupid thing to do, not because the above mentioned things are shamed by the society but because you are doing it out of peer pressure and not being yourself.

You can try to enjoy life or experience wild things but do it when you genuinely want to do it and not because you want to portray a certain image of yourself or want to fit in.

Another example of girls usually trying to be someone else other than their natural personalities is when they see an actress in some cheesy film or sitcom who is the "ultimate girl" – most desirable and prettiest, and often very mean and rude to girls who are not as pretty as her and mocking guys who are drooling over her. Just to attain that level of desirability and feel superior, many girls start behaving rudely and display bad attitude towards everyone and then consider themselves as "savage". Those girls are not cool at all; they are extremely irritating and lack basic manners. You will notice a lot of such girls (often lacking education and awareness) in small towns or in middle class families of metro cities, who have an "image" in their minds as to how rich and desirable girls behave and they mistake the coolness or spunky quotient with meanness.

I am sure you all have met such girls in your life. They often write things like "AtTiTuDe Gal" or "Ziddi Ladki" in their social media bios and take immense pride in insulting people because they think they are cool and desirable but in reality they are just a mess. Avoid being one of those. Understand that you are not good because you are beautiful, but you are beautiful because you are good.

Always fight for equality but don't become an extremist. Never indulge into male bashing and unreasonable comparisons.

Male-female arguments and who suffers more and who has more privileges is a never ending argument. Don't waste time in these unnecessary debates. Be independent, follow your heart and do what you feel is right for you. Focus on you career and goals. Be financially independent, no matter what. You may not have ambitions to earn millions but make sure you can support yourself without any financial assistance from others.

It will not only boost your self-confidence and morale but also ensure that you always have "a choice" to make your own decisions.

There are many women in our country who are in a toxic marriage and face constant physical, mental, emotional and psychological abuses and traumas but still they continue to stay with their partner simply because they are financial dependent on them and have nowhere else to go!

If they were financially independent, they would have a choice to get themselves out of their toxic marriage. Instead of looking for a rich man to be with, be rich yourself.

Moreover, even if you are in a happy marriage or your parents take care of all your expenses, it is extremely important to have your own financial independence and not be a "liability" on your partners or parents. They may never say it or make you feel like a liability, but it would be more convenient for them also if you can support yourself without their help.

Financial independence is not just about money but also about your identity. Being a CEO or director of a multinational corporation, a doctor, a painter, a teacher, a businesswoman, a gardener, a designer or any business or profession you are into, will give you immense satisfaction and a sense of individuality. It is good to be proud of your parents and partner and be associated with them but it is equally important to have an independent identity. It is better to let people introduce you as "She is ____ and she is a professional designer/accountant/doctor/lawyer etc." instead of just, "She is ____ and she is the daughter of ____/wife of ____".

Make sure you add some value to your relationship, if you want equality. If your partner picks and drops you everywhere, travels long distance to meet you, phone calls are as per only your schedule, they replace their family time or self-time with going out with you, they plan and pay for all your trips, dates and all you have to do is just show up, then it is not an equal relationship and you are not adding any value or contributing anything in your relationship.

I have seen many girls who are not grateful to their partners for doing everything for them. Instead, they keep excessively demanding more and more. They keep complaining about little things and are utterly ungrateful for their partner's efforts. I had interacted with one such guy who did everything for his partner but still she always cribbed.

He jokingly said, "I bet if Mumtaz was alive and saw the Taj Mahal (symbol of love), she still wouldn't be completely satisfied and complain about its marble quality or colour shade. Women always find some fault!"

Everybody laughed at that moment (again something I hate, men cracking women/wife jokes. So uncool), but then I actually witnessed many girls being ungrateful in spite of their own zero contribution in their relationship! I just hope you don't turn out that way.

Yes, set high standards, be upfront about things you dislike, give your honest opinions but also make sure that you contribute and add some value to the relationship. If your time and body is all you can give, then it is not value addition. Don't be that girl who would go on a date for "free food" instead of trying to know a person or have a good conversation. Don't be that girl who dates guys for all the "free stuff". An equal relationship is about taking turns to lean on each other and adding value to each other's life.

Just don't be the one who only provides her presence and receives a lot of privileges in return because such acts can also lead to unintentional male domination where men start controlling your life and take all decisions and when you ask for equality, they point out your zero contribution in the relationship and make you feel useless. It's better to live with pride, self-respect, dignity and as equals in relationships rather than being a parasite living on your partner's resources.

People often have a standard set as to how women should be, how they should behave, what should they wear and what should they be doing. For many individuals, the role of a woman is just to stay quiet and talk when asked something, be obedient, wear what they are asked to wear, give birth to children, do household work and spend their entire life "serving" men. Do not fall into the traps of stereotypes which the society has formed.

You are born to be yourself and do what you like (as long as it does not harm others), and not to match the standards set by the society or to impress anyone.

Just live your life the way you want, it is okay to wear whatever you like, it is okay to not know how to cook, it is okay if you don't want to marry until you yourself feel ready ("marry early or else you won't find a suitable match" is utter bullshit, marrying late is better than marrying wrong), it is okay if you don't want a child, it is okay if you follow your dreams instead of pampering egos of people around you. It is okay.

So, just live your life to the fullest and do what you want. You are not answerable to anyone for the choices you make for yourself.

It is also quite sad that these days many people blame women for rising divorce cases in our country.

I often hear people say things like "girls have become too selfish, ignorant etc.", some even say things like, "girls these days are spoilt and pampered so much that they are not wife material anymore", "financially independent girls are so focused on their careers and obsessed with money that they ignore relationships, "greedy parents of a money making girl are obsessed with money and hence don't want to marry off their daughters quickly", "modern day girls are influenced by the western culture of divorces."

I agree that our generation is not as patient as previous generations when it comes to relationships but blaming only women for it is absolutely wrong and unfair. It's not that women these days don't believe in marriage, but the fact is that modern day women ask for equal rights, equal power and equal responsibility which most old school men are unable to process and hence their fragile egos simply cannot handle a strong, independent and opinionated woman. This results into constant fights, domestic violence, all sorts of abuses resulting into separation.

There will be many of you who must have gone through some kind of sexual abuse or harassment in your life so far. It is extremely important to speak out. Movements like #MeToo and Time's Up have done much to draw attention to the reality which many of us already know, yet we brush it under the carpet. I would suggest you to speak up and also stand up for fellow women.

I have often noticed that many times women who sing praises of girl power, feminism and female friendship publicly, degrade fellow women in private and cause more harm to women. It is sad but true.

Often pretty girls mock girls who lack desirable features or often body shame other girls and make fun of their outfit or fashion sense much more than what men do.

I see so many girls who call themselves "best friends", rip each other apart in each other's absence and indulge in merciless gossiping. Unnecessary comparisons and competition among girls often leads to them putting each other down.

Moreover, I have actually witnessed traditional conservative girls passing sexist and derogatory remarks, or often slut shaming other girls who wear revealing clothes or any attractive girl who makes them insecure. In our country the daughter-in-law and mother-in-law are often back biting, pulling each other down and fighting for the attention and love of their husband/son instead of sharing love and living like a happy family. There are various other manners in which women are women's worst enemies.

This cannot be ignored and passed off as just "stereotypes" made by men. You might have actually experienced some incidences in your life as well. Therefore, it is better to uplift, encourage and positively promote each other and stand united against the patriarchal society instead of fighting with each other.

There are so many desperate men who try to approach a girl and are unable to accept rejection. Women are often blamed for their sudden mood swings but if you notice, nobody changes their mood and tone as quickly as a guy who has been rejected or ignored by a girl. From giving her compliments to woo her initially, now after rejection he starts calling her "slut" or tries to damage her reputation.

Most misogynistic men (and some women too) cannot digest the fact that a woman wants equality and therefore, women are called names and are often ridiculed in an attempt to silence them. The society will mock you when you try to defy their unreasonable and unfair rules. But you need to be brave, bold and fearless. Do what you like. Be yourself. To all the women labeled as:-

1. *"Aggressive", continue to be assertive,*

2. *"Greedy", continue to be ambitious,*

3. *"Bossy", keep on leading,*

4. *"Difficult", keep rejecting bull shit and continue to stand up for yourself,*

5. *"Complicated", continue to have independent opinions and views which may not be accepted (or understood) by the majority,*

6. *"Rebellious", continue to follow your heart and oppose suppression.*

Dear Brothers,

I started my letter for females with "hope you are doing well" and major part of the letter emphasized on how difficult and unfair the world has been to women and how much unequal distribution of power and opportunities is there in this male dominated world. When I introspect, I can't help but wonder that why didn't I naturally think of writing "hope you are doing well" for you as well? Then I suddenly realized my bias which has been ingrained in all of our heads since birth that, "men cannot afford to be not doing well." According to the society, guys are supposed to dominate the world and hence you should also take extra responsibility of everyone around you in order to enjoy and "deserve" the power you get irrespective of the fact whether you actually want that power or not. Males are expected to excel, irrespective of their will, skill or capability, in whatever they do. They are told that they should be the ones earning a lot of wealth for their parents, wife, children and sometimes even for future generations. Many of you are already suffering from the burden of your parent's dreams, your dreams and also dreams and expectations of irrelevant people like your neighbours or relatives. I know that the baggage of so many expectations and responsibilities is too heavy for your shoulders sometimes and you give your best to make everyone happy, even at the cost of your own happiness. It is normally expected from young men to succeed in life and take charge of the family.

Men are expected to do all the financial planning like make a fixed deposit, do proper investments, have a bank balance to buy a house, car and all the luxuries. Probably, this conditioning is the reason that when you go on dates, many girls expect you to pay the bill (their fault) but then there are also many self-respecting girls who prefer to share the bill and yet you feel the pressure (your fault) to pay the entire bill because you are a man and you "need to" pay for her and take her responsibility.

So, you aggressively insist on paying because it makes you feel "in control", dominating or you do it to avoid the "guilt" of taking money from a girl. This conditioning needs to change in order to have equality.

Another perception which you all constantly battle is "men are meant to be tough".

People sometimes keep preaching that men should cry and be more expressive, but the truth is that the moment you let your feelings out and seek emotional support you are considered weak. I think everyone should be allowed to be vulnerable since it is a basic human emotion. Also, the definition of "tough" and "strong" are often limited to strength and "control over emotions". Things like being physically strong, having a deep voice, being athletic, walking and talking in a "manly manner" or having facial hair does not define your masculinity.

Just like women face issues at work place, men also face a lot of problems. For example – For Chartered Accountants, September is one of the busiest months as September is the deadline for filing audit reports.

In one of the offices where I worked, I felt the inequality when girls were asked to leave at their regular time and boys were instructed to leave after 11pm because it is "unsafe" for women to travel at night. If we observe closely, this problem is also created by men only as many crimes against women including theft and rapes, take place at night time and hence it is not safe for women to walk alone on streets at night. Most of the unfair things happening to men are mostly because of the horrendous acts performed by other men. Another example would be that in case of any dispute between a male and a female, the girl is considered innocent and the guy is considered guilty by default, until proven otherwise. Even some of our laws are written in that fashion. Sadly, it is also fact that most crimes recorded officially are committed by men and therefore you also constantly battle the perception.

Saying "not all men" is not the only way to counter that. It is important to also speak up and take a stand for females and it all starts at your home.

Help your mother and sister, appreciate their work, encourage them to fully utilize their potential and follow their passion. Also, when you like a girl and get attracted to her, share your feelings in the most honest, humble and polite manner. Do not use coercive/aggressive methods or cheesy pickup lines which so called "heroes" use in films. It doesn't work in real life. A lot of guys (mostly uneducated, irrational or unaware) try to behave like the filmy heroes.

So, when they like a girl they stalk them, touch them without consent, and embarrass them publically by singing songs or mimicking them or writing something cheesy on the public walls, benches or their vehicles etc. I know a lot of people who strongly believe that "girls are shy so they never express their liking openly so even if she says no, it actually means a yes". This is infuriatingly idiotic! We boys have been made to believe that the girl first denies, then we have to "chase her", then she finally gives in and accepts us. This is not how things work. Moreover, respect her decision. If she says yes, great, but if she rejects you, don't take it personally. Don't try to spread rumours about her character or try to damage her reputation just because she rejected you.. "Real men can take a no for an answer."

The worst thing you can do is cause physical harm like raping her or throwing acid on her face, or assaulting her or her potential or current partner or her family members. Even if you get such thoughts (which you shouldn't get in the first place) then just calm down and think what if someone does the same to your sister and how adverse impact will it have on her and your entire family. Have empathy. Just accept her rejection and move on, you will find someone better. Take it as a motivation and learn to convert your weaknesses into your strengths.

Moreover, we are so used to being the one who controls and dominates everything that we sometimes tend to snatch freedom of our partner and we call it "protecting" them from harmful people.

It is a fact that we boys can easily decode the intentions of others boys more accurately than girls can and hence when a guy with bad intentions acts friendly with our unsuspecting partner, it is our responsibility to protect her. However, most of us start getting paranoid and insecure and we end up suffocating our partner. Every human being has the basic freedom to choose who their friends and colleagues will be and with whom they want to interact. You cannot order or instruct your girl that "don't talk to that guy" and misuse your control over her too liberally and excessively. Stay by her side, be there for her, protect her but also trust her and give her space to live her life with her own choices.

Because of many kinds of privileges and pampering which we have received in our childhood, we sometimes refuse to grow up.

We always want the things to be done our way. If we don't get what we want, most of the times we create havoc and get nasty.

It is high time that we lose our sense of entitlement and become more empathetic and caring towards people around us. Also, stop taking undue advantage of the old school male oriented traditions and learn to accept equality. For example – Stop taking dowry, no matter how qualified you are or whether you have a Government job or not. Just don't take it. You are in a way selling yourself. Many people are not even aware of what exactly is dowry. Anything given or taken by any party involving valuable security or any property moveable or immoveable, is dowry when it is without free will and consent.

It puts a lot of financial stress and burden on the bride's family. Women who can't pay an expected dowry price or who are unable to make additional payments in the future are often subjected to harassment and abuse. The dowry system casts women as a burden, rather than an asset, leading to female infanticide in many cases. The whole dowry system is just completely wrong!

Anything which has been followed since ages doesn't always mean it is correct. Just like the apps on our phones, we need to update our traditions with time as well. Also, I hear a lot of people say this which is annoying at times — "My parents asked for it, I didn't."

This cannot be an excuse! Convince your parents to not take dowry. Yes, if the parents of the bride willingly want to gift their daughter anything, one has to respect their sentiments as well. Make sure, whatever they gift, it is in the name and ownership of the bride only, always.

You may like it or not but you are expected to be successful in whatever field you are in. That's how a major part of the world works. So, start working hard. Stop wasting your precious time in liking semi-nude photos of Instagram models and commenting on their photos and reels or randomly sending requests/messages to girls and instead start working towards achieving your goals. You will get all the female attention as a by-product once you are successful. The bitter truth of life is that people respect and get attracted to only successful people. Just think about any successful person that you admire and visualize their appearance before and after they are successful.

Success not only gives you money but also gets you an alluring aura, a glow on your face and a confidence in your personality which attract a lot of people.

We all have had fantasies of being a Casanova or to have multiple girlfriends at some point in our lives. Some guys still have such desires but let me honestly tell you that unless you are already famous or you come from a wealthy family, you cannot have a wild dating life in your youth and at the same time achieve something big and get successful, it is impossible. Excessive dating and having multiple partners can lead to a lot of distraction (which you will love to have at that moment) and make you lose your focus from your goals. Moreover, you might have many flings but ultimately you will be tagged as "not a husband material" and girls will eventually distance themselves from you because of your reputation of being a womanizer.

You will never be able to settle with one person and end up being lonely and empty. Don't waste your youth in chasing girls, spend your precious time in achieving big things, making yourself and your parents proud, securing your and your family's future, helping people as much as possible and performing good karmas, and gaining a lot of amazing life experiences. Success is not always about how much money you have but make sure you earn sufficient amount of money. Don't let idealistic philosophers confuse you into believing that money doesn't matter. In the world we live in, it does.

Money cannot buy happiness but it can give you immense satisfaction when you can help people with your money, it can give you enjoyable pleasures of life by ensuring that you can buy your favourite cars, a good house, eat delicious exotic food, wear good clothes, give good education to your children, provide the best medical facilities to your loved ones, give a comfortable life to your family and all these things are a part of happiness. Just don't be so greedy about money that you lose your mental peace and forget to appreciate the existence of your loved ones and also to enjoy the money that you have already earned. Finally to conclude this letter, I would just like to say that don't fall for gender stereotypes. If you feel like crying, cry your heart out. If you like a Pink shirt at the shopping mall, buy it and wear it unapologetically. If your young boy wants to play with dolls instead of guns, give him what he likes.

If you can solve any issue with calmness then avoid unnecessary aggression and violence to prove your "manliness". If you don't like to watch or play sports, it's completely fine. If you are passionate about activities like dancing, cooking, fashion designing or anything else, follow that. It's okay if you are not muscular. It's okay if you like to wax your body, have long hair, paint your nails, use hairbands, wear jewellery and apply make-up. Instead of following the standards set by the society, live by your own definition of what modern manhood is about.

CHAPTER 10

"IMPORTANT TRENDING TOPICS"

At the end of the book, let's open our hearts (and minds) and bluntly talk about some trending and perhaps uncomfortable topics which are usually brushed under the carpet. Unfortunately, such topics do not form part of the day to day conversations in our social circle. I personally believe that we should be able to discuss anything and everything with at least people of our inner circle. It will not only give you a different perspective but will also provide much needed knowledge and awareness about certain things. It will also enable you to introspect and ask yourself some very critical questions.

Normally, I notice a lot of confusion among the youth today about their attraction to people other than their partner. As discussed earlier in chapter four, it is natural to get attracted to someone outside your relationship. If you act on it without your partner's knowledge, it is called infidelity. But there can be few other possibilities which depend on the *"consent"* of your partner.

What if your partner is okay with you having a romantic relationship with someone else? What if you realize that you are capable of being attracted to more than one person? Well, the answer to that is that you want a non-monogamous relationship. Monogamy is still very much the norm in today's societies, but different types of romantic relationships are gaining acceptance globally. Many people get confused between *polyamory, polygamy, polygyny, and polyandry* — and this confusion is understandable, considering that these terms are new to most of us! But is the concept of Polygamy actually new?

Polygamy is not a new concept at all. In fact, we as humans lived in a polygamous state throughout the history of mankind. Only in recent centuries, the concept of monogamy became more popular when ideas about *"loyalty"* and *"settling down"* gained recognition.

Non-monogamous relationships comprise of different relationship styles that involve more than two people, but there are some key differences between them. Polyamory is the act of having intimate relationships with more than one person at the same time. A polyamorous person has multiple romantic partners. Polygamy, on the other hand, involves being married to multiple partners. Some polyamorous people are married and have partners outside of their marriage. However, polygamy exclusively describes relationships where people are *"married"*. Polygyny specifically refers to a man who has multiple wives. Polyandry refers to a woman who has multiple husbands. Polyamory and polygamy are both gender-neutral terms.

They can refer to women having multiple partners of any gender, men having multiple partners of any gender, or non-binary people having partners of any gender. There is a misconception that polyamorous people are only polyamorous because they cannot commit or don't want to settle down.

This isn't true — in fact, they are open to committing to multiple partners!

There can be many reasons to try non-monogamous relationships.

Some of them are listed below :-

1. Either you or your primary partner feel attracted to others while still feeling attracted to each other,

2. Your partner or you want to *"love"* multiple people at the same time,

3. You might want to experience romance with someone of a different gender than your partner,

4. Simply because the idea of dating multiple people feels exciting, liberating and appealing to you.

5. You are interested in experimenting out of curiosity.

The difference between polyamory and cheating is of consent. If your partner gives you their consent to have other partners, it is not cheating, it is polyamory. However, there can be certain restrictions put by a partner.

For example, if your partner only consents you to get involved with people they know, and you secretly get involved with someone they don't know, then it is a form of cheating.

Monogamy is not the only way to have a relationship. If you are interested in polyamory, you should talk to your current partner about it. Be honest and upfront. It is quite common for many people to feel like they are *"not enough"* when their partner brings up an interest in non-monogamy, which is a totally valid feeling. It is your responsibility to emphasize and explain them why you are interested in ethical non-monogamy. Remind them that it is not because you don't love them or aren't satisfied with them.

Like any other kind of relationship, non-monogamous relationships also come with some disadvantages and drawbacks. Apart from the media representation and social stigma, non-monogamous relationships can also have issue of jealousy. However, it can be avoided if the partner is great at continually showing affection and care to the primary partner and respects their feelings. Healthy polyamorous relationships are based on good time management skills and great communication.

One thing which I have often noticed about polygamy is that this concept promotes gender inequality. In fact, in regions where men have multiple wives, those wives often only have confined rights. In turn, those wives often don't have the opportunity to educate themselves and to work in a profession they like. Instead, they often have to stay at home and have to cook and do the household work.

Women in polygamous relationships are also at an elevated risk of physical and psychological harm. They face higher rates of domestic violence and abuse, including sexual abuse. Competition for material and emotional access to a shared husband can lead to fractious co-wife relationships. If you want to be a member of the polyamorous community you need to be extra careful about pre-screening your partners. You have to explore their emotional intelligence and how this person handles jealousy.

If you are already in a relationship, a new partner has to integrate well into that pre-existing partnership. It is also equally important to filter out people who would use such relationships as an excuse to exploit and abuse others.

Although there are no pre-defined rules and ranks in a poly relationship, there is still going to be a tendency for one partner to get more out of the relationship than the others. This means that there is always going to be a bit of unfairness and inequality going on, and that often will result in people trying to *"steal"* time or resources from other people – either intentionally or unintentionally. For some, this can lead to a phenomenon of being dumped with little to no warning from others, over the smallest of transgressions.

One of the risks attached to Polygamous relationships is that it spreads diseases especially Sexually Transmitted Diseases like HIV aids, significantly.

I am not here to take sides and tell you whether you should be in a monogamous or a non- monogamous relationship.

It is your choice. I am here to give you an accurate awareness about different possibilities which you may or may not indulge into. Therefore, everyone should decide for themselves (along with a discussion with their partner) whether a polygamous lifestyle is suitable for them or if they rather want to spend their lives with only one partner peacefully.

However, at the risk of sounding old fashioned, I personally believe that every person should seek a single soul or have only one romantic partner at a time, in order to bring stability, peace and joy to their relationship. The funny thing about poly relationships is that they often make you see people as disposable. When you always have another option, you stop putting in the amount of effort you should put into a relationship. It tends to bring out the worst in you. Instead of trying to fight for a relationship, you will end up flippantly shrugging off issues and running off to another partner just because you can, and because it is harder to care about people when you can easily throw them away and get a replacement.

Many intellectuals have stated that human beings are naturally polyamorous, but when it actually comes to settling down, we all want to come home to someone who sees us as our *"one and only"*.

> *"Instead of loving multiple partners, love your partner in multiple ways."*

Hookups are becoming more engrained in popular culture, reflecting both evolved sexual predilections and changing social and sexual scripts. However, these encounters often transpire without any promise of or desire for a more traditional romantic relationship.

This normalization of sexual desires allows the topic of sex into a daily conversation among adolescents in ways that have been a taboo in the past.

Hookup culture has become more integrated in popular culture in a monetized way, like through mobile apps, movies and songs which normalize casual sexual relations between strangers.

I have observed that many people feel degraded, guilty or *"feel cheap"* after hooking up with a stranger or a friend. This feeling is mainly observed more among the females compared to their male counterpart.

After various interactions with such females, I realized that the reason they felt degraded or cheap wasn't because casual sex is inherently degrading or immoral but because their hookup partners treated them like an object. Their hook up partners didn't care about their pleasure, disrespected and ignored them afterwards, and were often pushy and coercive.

Even when women ask for what they want, their male hookup partners may not always care enough to "make an effort". Now let's hear the male's perspective. One such guy said that he is not going to try as hard as when he is with someone he *"really cares about."* In few cases, there also have been women who have used men and treated them like objects for their pleasure and dumped them later without any explanation or warning. That is why it is best to be on the same page and set your expectations in sync with your hook up partner. Contrary to the common belief, even men may face adverse situations due to hookups.

Men who are a sexual, have low sex drives, prefer intimacy only in committed relationships, or feel too shy to initiate foreplay are seen as less *"manly"* and are often ridiculed by other men (and sometimes by women, too). Hook-up scenarios may include feelings of pressure and performance anxiety, contributing to feelings of discomfort.

Another major problem in the hookup culture, faced especially by women is their character assassination by the judgmental men and women of the regressive society.

I have seen so many men who pursue women and try to convince them to get intimate – sometimes even using coercion – and then later turn around and call them sluts for agreeing.

All women should always remember that you never deserve ridicule or disrespect for choosing to get intimate with someone who wants to get intimate with you. It doesn't matter how recently you met or if you knew them before.

The *"rules"* for a stereotypical hookup are simple: No feelings. Don't get attached. Don't be jealous when they sleep with someone else. Don't be awkward or insecure about intimacy. Don't act like you are all that into them, or want to see them all that much. Don't get upset if they don't text again. Wait, that doesn't sound so simple after all?

While the idea that hookups can't include any actual emotions is ostensibly meant to keep things fun and easy for everyone, the amount of emotional self-policing involved can actually get pretty exhausting. However, for many people, physical intimacy does cause emotions – sometimes positive, sometimes negative and it is completely normal. Despite its increasing social acceptability, however, developing research suggests that hookups may leave more strings attached than many participants assume. It can deepen pre-existing attachments or cause new ones to form. You can still choose to keep things casual even if you have feelings for someone, or you can talk to them to see if they might be interested in making the relationship more serious. Hookups can also sometimes result in regret, guilt and negative feelings when things don't turn out as planned or expected by either of the parties.

Whatever opinion (liberal or traditional) one has about hookup culture, it is irrefutable that it has significantly changed the way that we think, act, and speak about sex.

Sex is no longer the unmentionable term that was only discussed behind closed doors, and the decisions of individuals to have sexual encounters are often no longer vilified as they were in the past.

Normalization of sex, an effect of hookup culture, has shaped our principles to be more accepting of physical intimacy and sexual diversity.

Unlike our previous generations, we have known about sex at a very early age — thanks to Biology classes and more importantly porn.

With such an easy access to the internet these days from their smart phones, most teenagers discover and learn about sex through porn even before their parents or teachers can educated them in the right manner. It is harmful and can easily misguide them at their curious, tender and impressionable age. This is why this taboo topic is included in this book, so that young readers can understand it holistically with its pros and cons.

Most people irrespective of their age have watched porn, some watch it regularly, and some don't. Porn is a double edged sword. For some it is just an art form. For some it can be informative. For some it can also be misleading. We need to have the ability to distinguish between porn's depictions of human body and sex and the everyday life of an average person. Many people are afraid and anxious that things they have seen in porn are expected of them. Pornography allows for a heightened sense of arousal, which may not actually be possible in real life. It also increases your personal knowledge about sexuality (sexual positions, attire, role-play, and the use of accessories). Porn may also facilitate arousal for individuals and couples who are looking to heat things up. Pornography can also be used for self-pleasuring in the absence of a partner. Men and women perceive and use porn differently, with men being six times more likely to consume it than women.

On the negative side, pornography may have men viewing women in a sexually derogatory manner. Also, it gives an unrealistic portrayal of human body and can sometimes make a person feel insecure or uncomfortable in their own skin. Pornography creates a contrast effect.

Many individuals begin to compare their partner's body and sexual performance with that of a porn star which is dangerous.

It can also be extremely addictive and people can have withdrawal symptoms when they are not able to watch porn on regular basis. Therefore, consume it, at your own risk.

Parents of teenagers need to ensure that they provide responsible *"sex education"* to their children so that they don't end up getting mislead or abused. Parents also need to teach their kids about "good touch" and "bad touch" to prevent child abuse. If your kid constantly rejects being with a particular individual (be it your relative or friend), there are chances that your kid is not comfortable with the touch or vibe of that individual. Do not force your kid to interact or be with that individual. If at any point of time, your son or daughter tells you that he/she has been molested or touched inappropriately by anyone, please be empathetic, compassionate towards your child and take strict action against the predator. Do not brush it under the carpet or try to convince your child that what happened to them should be kept a secret or forgotten or it was just a normal incident and they should not overreact as your lack of support can have a detrimental effect on your child.

Whenever we think of meeting someone special, we imagine fantastical scenarios which we have watched in rom-coms or read in books.

Imagine meeting your partner for the first time on a beautiful hill station while you are on a trekking trip, or accidently bumping into someone at a wedding, shopping mall or a movie theatre, getting introduced to a gorgeous looking person by your best friend in a birthday party or simply meeting someone special at a bar.

With each passing day, the possibility of such scenarios is getting reduced. Today it is common to hear that people prefer to find connections through dating apps, right at their fingertips on a mobile screen. So what is the likelihood of finding a long-term partner in the analogue world, especially for a cohort that has grown up glued to smartphones and with far more limited traditional interactions with strangers compared to previous generations?

We shop online, order transportation and food online and chat with friends online. Do most of us even know how to approach people we fancy in public these days?

Instead of going on multiple dates with various people, there are multiple matches waiting to be texted. Additionally, a good pick-up line doesn't hold quite the same zing when sent online, that too with emojis. When a date doesn't go well or a text conversation turns bland, one simply un-matches and forgets the existence of that person.

Dating apps have their pros and cons. For socially awkward, anxious or shy people, trying to meet a stranger in public is a nightmare, and even for someone charming and outgoing, it is a gruelling task that requires a lot of preparation and luck.

Hence, such dating apps are useful to meet new people. It saves time and energy. Also, there are very limited options for people wanting to date without an online medium. Other than high school, college or work or through a friend, there really isn't any way else. Besides, living in a small town is even worse.

It is unlikely to find your soul mate in the same town where you live; you have to expand your horizons. Many people these days think it is better to search for partners online. It also gives them a lot of choices.

The cons of dating apps are many as well.

A lot of dating apps are filled with a lot of fake profiles. Secondly, even after going through hundreds of profiles, once you find a decent match it is extremely difficult to stay in touch because the *"attention span"* of our generation is extremely low. So, when conversations unexpectedly fizzle, people are quick to un-match and ghost you! Moreover, in spite of chatting for many hours or days, if the sparks don't translate in-person, the dates can be quite insulting when people just shamelessly leave after few minutes without thinking about the impact of their action on you. Apart from that, there are so many other issues like misleading profiles, safety concerns, derogatory comments and unwanted explicit content. I am sure many of you (especially girls) must have received unwanted explicit pictures or videos via dating apps or social media.

Some people say dating apps are useful because they make sure that nobody is lonely. I think that is a wrong perception.

In fact, users who easily get attached after chatting regularly end up feeling lonelier than they did in the first place since most dating app matches might disappear without warning due to various reasons. Ghosting and lack of transparency are big concerns of online dating apps.

Most people don't look like their pictures which are often edited. Good first dates that don't lead to anything more serious is the most frequent irritation, which can feel like a waste of effort and can lead to frustration. Also, people have grown so used to meeting partners online that they end up ignoring potential matches elsewhere.

Matching frequently with random people can build up some self-confidence, but that same confidence can be smashed when someone you don't even know doesn't swipe right for you or ignores your messages. We connect our self-worth with the opinions of people we might not ever meet, which is extremely hazardous.

The element of humanity has sadly been replaced with technology these days. Your actual and virtual personalities are two different things. It is impossible to sum up all the brilliant, complex, weird, goofy and vulnerable parts of yourself in handful photos, bios, captions and emojis. It is important to understand that whether people are swiping right or left on your profile, it is not a complete invitation or rejection of your full, embodied self. Don't forget that you are so much more than pixels on a screen.

"You are a person and not a profile."

The world of online dating has some incredible benefits and might lead to real relationships, but at what cost?

Our generation has begun to sacrifice the essential components that make us social creatures. We have sacrificed safety and reality for convenience.

I don't believe that dating apps are inherently bad, but it is time we take a closer look at how they affect us. Online dating is sometimes not worth the price we pay.

Still if you want to use dating apps, here are few *"dating app tips"* which you should follow in order to successfully attract the right people to your profile.

1. Have minimum 3-4 pictures of yourself (preferably solo pictures). Keeping just one photo is not convincing. People want to see more of you and how you look from different angles, to form a judgment of your appearance.

2. PLEASE avoid photos where you are wearing sun glasses! It's an idiotic thing to do. Eyes reveal a lot about a person and are necessary to see through your personality.

3. Use minimum filters. It will ensure that people who like you, like you for your actual looks. If you use filters to enhance your appearance, then you may match with a lot of people but when you meet them, they will surely be disappointed and your date can be disastrous.

4. Don't have all your pictures in the same outfit. I know that when you dress amazingly for an event (like a wedding or a party), you look really dazzling and you click a lot of pictures of yourself in different poses but choose any one of them for your profile. Repetition of those incredible photos in the same outfit tones down their worth.

5. Avoid using cheesy pickup lines and inappropriate language.

6. Write an honest bio. No exaggeration. No underplaying. Just exactly the reality.

Another thing that I have noticed a lot among people is their ignorance about the LGBTQIA+ communities. Most people often mock, avoid, disrespect, fear or abuse people from LGBTQIA communities because they have no knowledge about them. One of the objectives of writing this book for me is also to make my readers aware about the importance to acknowledge and promote diversity and inclusion of every individual irrespective of their caste, gender and sexual orientation. Therefore, the content of this book can also be applied in the lives of a lesbian, gay, bisexual, transgender, queer, intersex and asexual/agender person. The terms lesbian, gay, bisexual and pansexual refer to people's sexual orientation, that is, who they experience sexual attraction towards, while transgender refers to gender identity, that is, *"someone whose gender differs from the one they were given when they were born"*.

Terms like gender queer and non-binary refer to people who fall outside the construction of gender as male or female. Intersex people are born with physical or biological sex characteristics such as reproductive or sexual anatomy, hormones or chromosomes that do not seem to fit the typical definitions of female or male.

I cannot emphasis enough to let my readers know that such people are naturally born this way.

Contrary to the conservative conclusions, they are neither influenced by the *"Western culture"* nor are they sick or need medical attention. They are just normal people like we all are - they feel love, sadness, anger, jealousy, kindness and every other emotions which any of us generate, they have similar ambitions to earn well, have friends and family who love and support them, follow their hobbies and passions etc.

LGBTQIA people are entitled to the enjoyment of all the rights outlined in international, regional and domestic human rights law. Yet, due to strongly held cultural and social norms surrounding gender expression and sexuality, LGBTQIA people are often excluded and they constantly battle fear, inequality, injustice, hatred and many other issues which normally a person should not face based on who they love or the way they are born. I am sure most of you in your childhood got afraid of eunuchs when they came to ask for money in trains or at a signal point. because you were simply unaware about them.

Dear reader, if you are from the LGBTQIA group, then I can only assume how difficult life has been for you. From accepting yourself to being victims of discrimination, being subject to slurs or jokes or suffering rejection by a family member, life has been tough. Another issue is when gender-minority individuals enter a gender-homogeneous workplace, they face a heightened probability of experiencing *"tokenism"*. It refers to the practice of making only a perfunctory or symbolic effort to do a particular thing, especially by recruiting a small number of people from under-represented groups in order to give the appearance of sexual or racial equality within a workforce.

I don't want to show you sympathy and make you feel bitter and victimized; you are much stronger than that. You don't need sympathy, all you need is empathy and to be treated with equal rights.

However, let me tell you that god has made you special, don't try to fit in when you are meant to stand out.

Accept yourself first. It would be impractical for me to tell you to *"come out of the closet"* without knowing your circumstances. However, it will be more liberating if you *"come out"* and have friends and family who love and accept you for who you are. Some may resist you for a while, some may stop talking to you...well their loss.

When you are true to yourself you will attract people who are genuinely meant to be in your life.

Don't let anyone tell you or make you believe that *"You are not normal, or you are sick", "You are just confused", "This is a disease, you need a cure", "Homosexuality in general is a foreign import, not part of the traditional culture", "This is just a phase"* or *"You are committing a sin".*

Although times are changing and things are improving in many parts of the world thanks to social media awareness, inclusion programs, modifications of rigid laws etc. However, there are still so many things which need improvement. The common issue I find with the gender equality, gender management and gender mainstreaming approaches is that they very ignorantly overlook most problems faced by the "minorities" in the LGBTQIA community especially women, people from marginalized caste, colour, creed and religion. I have attended many LGBTQIA functions and events during my college social work projects and have observed that most of the spokespersons of the LGBTQIA community were males! The females are less in number and are away from the mainstream lime light. It is essential to have equality even within the LGBTQIA community in order to maximize efforts in negotiating equal human rights for them. These problems seem to originate in the neoliberalization of former radical movements when adopted by the mainstream. This translates into actions addressing sexism and heterosexism that overlook other forms of discrimination (e.g., racism, untouchability, and prejudice against a particular caste or religion).

Another thing which I have noticed a lot is exploitation of the LGBTQIA communities by the corporates brands. Many companies are supporting the LGBTQIA communities in various ways.

However, there are also some corporate brands (Google them), who don't do anything for the LGBTQIA community for the entire year or have strong associations with countries with anti-LGBTQIA laws or with individuals who are LGBTQIA phobic and only during the "Pride Month" in June, they change their logos to rainbow colours to show their symbolic support to the community but their real intention is only to get the marketing and advertising boost from their campaign. Such temporary, commercialized and fake support for the LGBTQIA communities is ubiquitous as some companies who are promoting LGBTQIA Pride — and ostensibly cashing in on Pride merchandise or retail — aren't doing much for the LGBTQIA community beyond contributing to this vague notion of spreading "awareness". It is nominal activism divorced from real action. I also encourage all my readers to make sure you buy products from only those companies who genuinely care for the LGBTQIA community — check their donations amount, get to know about how fair, inclusive and equal their corporate policies are, verify with whom they collaborate and get associated etc.

Every individual from the dominant group should recognize that their privilege should be shared and it is important to promote kindness and equality for those who don't possess that privilege.

Lesbian, gay, bisexual, transgender, queer, intersex, asexual/agender (LGBTQIA) people only want equal rights, not special rights.

"The status of the LGBTQIA community is a good litmus test for the status of human rights in a society."

Now let's talk about one of the most misunderstood words that I have come across recently, which is *"feminism"*. I have actually seen many men put up matrimonial ads in newspapers or websites which clearly state that the girl "should not be a feminist"!

People generally associate the term with females who love to indulge in male bashing and consider themselves superior than men or who want "special privileges" because they are females.

They are often called *"feminazi"* on social media by authoritarian extremists for whom the talk of equality is too much to swallow, but I prefer not to use that derogatory term. Instead, they should be called *"misguided feminists"* who strongly believe in male bashing, female superiority and often use sayings like *"what men can do, women can do better"* which promote a different kind of inequality. I feel that one should never associate any skill or talent with a gender; it all depends on each individual.

If you closely observe, you will find many misguided feminists hiding behind the mask of feminists and in a way tarnishing the holy movement of feminism and equality because of their irrationality and radicalism.

Such misguided feminists are in every field, film actresses (especially the unsuccessful ones who have small achievements and bigger opinions), journalists, sports, politics, business etc. who in a way make a "much needed" conversation about women empowerment and equality unpopular among the common public because of their illogical extremism, selfish propaganda and single dimensional perspective. Some females have become this extreme perhaps because of their bitter past experiences with few men (which does not give them right to degrade all men) and some strongly believe (rightly so) that females have been oppressed since many centuries by men and now they want (very wrongly so) revenge for it from all the men existing today!

They believe it is payback time and role reversal should happen where "strong" and "fiery" females will dominate and suppress all men around them (even those who have always been gentle and kind). I am not even joking, I have actually heard many women who claim to be feminists, say such silly things to provoke unsuspecting young girls.

Another type is those who play the victim card to justify their wrong actions. I have personally witnessed an incident where one such misguided feminist slapped her boyfriend during a heated argument and when he slapped her back, she said *"how can a man hit a girl?"* and argued unsuccessfully by giving statements like, *"men have more strength, so one slap of a girl and one slap of a guy are not the same, the guy should be punished."* I mean seriously?

Yes, it can be true that generally men have more strength but a slap is a slap. Men may feel less physical pain by a female slap but the humiliation it causes and the harm it can have on his self-esteem cannot be ignored.

Therefore, nobody irrespective of their gender should use violence and if they do and the other person retaliates, don't complain. Such misguided feminists misrepresent feminism's goals of equality and misuse the word *"feminism"* as a symbol of a radical culture. At the end of the day, if your idea of feminism tries to exclude anyone for gender purposes or race or any other identifying features, it is not real feminism. If it scapegoats ANYONE because of their skin, religion, gender identity, sexuality, etc. it is not real feminism.

Real feminism is bringing everyone together, to achieve a better future so that **everyone** can live in a world with "equal" privileges, freedom and opportunities and no one gets to dominate or exploit anyone because of their gender. Everyone has a part to play in the feminist movement.

"Feminism is about equality, not just in sharing power but also in sharing responsibility and accountability."

In present time we spend so many hours on social media. If we use it in a constructive manner, social media has many advantages. We know more things and have a deeper knowledge of the current affairs than what our previous generations had when they were our age. Social media keeps us updated about everything and also helps us in learning new skills. It also enables us to stay *"in touch"* with the world.

The internet and social media provide us with a range of benefits and opportunities to empower ourselves in various manner. Many people have successfully monetized social media by becoming influencers or promoting their business, products or their own skills and talent on social media. People can maintain social connections and support networks that otherwise wouldn't be possible, and can access more information than ever before. If nothing else, one can see and exchange memes for fun! However, social media websites are becoming notorious for cyber bullying and excessive trolling at an alarming rate. Merciless trolling can scar some people for life. Therefore, you should ensure that you don't waste your time and energy in trolling people.

You may find someone with a different political or religious ideology or find someone whose favourite actor/team/comics/sportsperson/politician is someone you dislike, but you should never write mean and hurtful messages just because you don't agree with their choice or ideology. It is a complete waste of time.

"Having difference of opinion does not mean being enemies."

For example, if you are not happy with your government and someone supports the government, it doesn't mean that you should hate that person or pass personal remarks at them. I see so many people fighting over political issues across the globe. It is the right of every citizen to critique its government when they are not satisfied with their performance.

It is admirable when the youth of the country takes interest in politics but one should have a <u>balanced point of view</u>.

You need to praise and support your government when they do good work and hold them accountable for their inefficiencies. But if you don't agree with someone's opinion, you cannot harass or bully them! All the political parties have their own "paid IT cells" that troll their dissenters; you don't need to be a part of their (unpaid) "army". Also, focus on the issues and not on individuals. You may break your friendship with your best friend or your romantic connection over political disagreements but the one you are blindly fighting for are often "acquaintances" of each other after all. If you closely observe, all the politicians irrespective of their different parties/ideologies are always cordial with each other (except during elections) and often go to each other's parties, events, functions, marriage of each other's children etc. and here you are fighting with your close ones for them. Similarly, your favourite actor and your friend's favourite actor may be rivals professionally, but they will always be cordial with each other. Same thing with sportspersons. Ronaldo and Messi will always respect and praise each other but their blind fans will fight over who is better.

"Never be a blind follower or a blind hater."

Interact more with people with a different thought process, it will enable you to grow and expose you to different perspectives.

I also find a lot of youngsters in a dilemma about *"freedom"* and *"independence"*. Since we all are exposed to the western culture and are highly influenced by them, we have become a strange hybrid of our culture and theirs. We aspire to follow their standard of living because we think they live a better life than us. In some ways they do but it's important to stay rooted and also know your culture. Don't be an orthodox, rigid, blind follower of traditions and social norms but at the same time, try to hold onto the good things from our vast and diverse culture.

In the west, most children leave their parent's house when they turn 18, some even earlier. We think living alone is fun and they have absolutely no restrictions.

We see social media pictures of our friends who live abroad and think that they are having so much fun. They can bring anyone home at any time, drink, party, chill and do everything they want without any accountability but we ignore that how difficult it is to survive alone and clear bills, take care of the house, clean it, do your own laundry, wash your clothes and dishes, manage your safety, handle loneliness and single handedly pay for all the expenses. We only see the "fun side" of living alone and keep fighting with our parents for freedom.

Many of you might have watched movies and sitcoms where young people live together and have the best time of their lives but they certainly don't show the harsh realities of staying without family. A lot of wealthy people who have moved to different places to study claim they love being alone but they are the ones who enjoy only the privileges and their parents send them money and pay for everything.

If you want to grow as an individuals and become independent, then surely living alone is a good move but if having fun or living a fantasy sitcom/movie kind of life is the objective then you might get a hard hitting reality check soon.

In the West, people prefer to have space and privacy and lead individualistic lifestyle. A normal average man and woman might have gone through divorces, might have children with multiple partners and marry multiple times and have a family gathering just once or twice a year.

Everyone lives their own life without depending on each other. However, our culture is more family oriented. We share everything. We eat, watch movies, go for trips and share many life experiences with our family. I have many American and British friends and they take prior "appointments" on Sundays from their parents to meet them. Here, it's totally opposite - we meet our friends on weekends to party and stay with our parents every day.

It is good to be independent but don't be ashamed of living or going out with your parents. I observe a lot of young people get embarrassed to spend time with their parents or to introduce them to their friends. Parents give us birth and sacrifice so many things for us and we conveniently avoid them once we become adults. _It is completely okay_ if we live with our parents at their expense till we complete our education and start earning and perhaps even after that. Don't stress yourself too much and make sure that when your parents get old, you take care of them as well.

In the West, most young adults prefer to live independently, study at their own expense, work part time and do small jobs, pay their own insurance and student loan and all other expenses.

So, the next time you don't get permission from your parents to go for a trip or late night parties or call your friends for a night stay, and you think it's better to stay alone or stay in a different country, think holistically from every aspect. You need your parents more than they need you and it will always be like that. If you don't value your parents till they are alive, you will eventually realize their importance once they are gone and you will be filled with regret and sadness. Parents are everything. They may not always agree or understand your perspective, there might always be a generational gap between you and your parents but they are the only ones who will accept you with all your flaws and will support you unconditionally. It's okay if they don't know how to use the latest technology or have some conservative thoughts, don't insult them. Educate them. Be patient with them. They were also patient with you when you were young and repeatedly asked silly questions or constantly made the same mistakes again and again.

You spending some time with them is all they want from you. Show them that you love and value them.

Be with them and see the smile on their face. Knowing that your parents are happy and smiling because of you is the best feeling ever. It will give you immense happiness and satisfaction.

Yes, I know this book was supposed to be about relationships. Let's get back to our main topic. So, by now you would have got a better perspective of "the reality of love and relationships". If while reading this book, you have related your life with it, agreed to many things and also disagreed with some due to difference of opinion, then congratulations — you have actually connected and "lived through" my book.

The only thing that I want to add now is that, once you have found a good compatible person and you are in a stable, successful and happy relationship, stop looking for *"someone better"*. I know a lot of people who constantly keep trying to find someone better than their partner. Trust me, it is a never ending process. You will always find someone richer, more good looking, more successful, more attractive, more intelligent and better behaved than your current partner. Don't fall in that trap! Let me warn you, you will be tempted to change your partner and be with that "better" individual but then after some time you will come across someone even "better" than them. You will never be able to enjoy a stable relationship if you keep switching partners.

The "connect" and chemistry which you have with your partner can never be replaced with temporary attractive things like "appearance" and "wealth".

Another thing which I notice a lot is parents pressurizing their kids to get married even when they are not ready. In our country, approximately 90% of the people have arranged marriages. You will also be pressurized by your parents, relatives or friends for arranged marriage soon.

Many of you are already facing the pressure from everyone.

Not just from others, when you scroll through your social media, you will see many of your classmates or colleagues getting married, and you might feel left out. But then, is arranged marriage a good thing?

Well, it is popularly believed that arranged marriages have more success rate than love marriages.

The statistics of the divorce rate of arranged versus love marriage, also back that belief. However, this was an accurate trend for the previous generations.

Today's youth want a lot of things and are not ready to compromise. The steps that lead to marriage are as follows :-

1. You are attracted to a person and their personality interests you.

2. You get to know each other as friends.

3. You start having a romantic equation.

4. You get to know them deeper, more intimately and share your deepest feelings and thoughts with each other.

5. You become physically and emotionally close.

6. You fall in love after knowing them properly.

7. You check your compatibility with your partner.

8. Finally, you mutually decide to spend the rest of your lives together.

Most people I know skip these steps as per their convenience. Some directly want to get physically intimate, some directly want to fall in love and some are way too quick to marry only to regret it later. Arranged marriages might work as per popular beliefs. Some people do it because they are unable to find a perfect match for them on their own while others do it out of social pressures from family, relatives or friends. I personally find it very strange to marry a person whom you don't know completely or to judge them in few meetings or in few weeks.

On top of that, we have our values and morals like not engaging in pre-marital sex or discussing certain topics. If you don't get intimate with the person you are gonna marry, then how will you get to know your sexual compatibility? What if the girl you marry, is really bad at love making or what if the guy turns out to be impotent or secretly gay who is marrying you because of family pressure?

Surely, impotency or being a low performer in bed is not a bad trait and doesn't make people "incompatible" but the question here is to know pretty much every important detail about a person before marrying them. If a guy is impotent and the girl knows this and still wants to marry him because he is a wonderful guy, then it is completely alright. I would again like to give a friendly reminder that I am not here to tell you which is better and what you should do, I am only here to give you a realistic portrayal of various possibilities and eventually you get to decide what action you wish to take.

You may have a great marriage or a terrible marriage in both arranged marriage and love marriage scenarios respectively.

We all want to be with good people but we seldom make efforts to become good ourselves. We keep judging and giving away *"certificates"* to people in spite of not knowing their circumstances or about their problems. *For example* – a 17 year old girl who has got pregnant is judged by everyone but may be her lover betrayed her or she was raped. A guy who smokes and drinks a lot is not as bad as he is portrayed by the neighbours. Maybe, he has lost someone and has found peace in escaping the reality with the help of cigarettes or alcohol. As long as people consume things which are legal, you are nobody to judge their personality. Smoking and drinking is bad for your health, not character. If we don't know the details, we shouldn't come to quick conclusions. Avoid listening to or spreading lies and rumours about anyone. Moreover, stop judging people by the stereotypes.

It is not guaranteed that a person who regularly visits temple, church or a mosque, or doesn't smoke or drink is a good human being; he may indulge in frauds or violence. A girl with tattoos, piercings and a rebellious attitude might actually be good at heart. Never judge a book by its cover is such an apt quote to live a proper life. If you want to judge someone then judge them on correct basis like how they treat others, their kindness and honesty, their intentions etc. However, instead of wasting time in judging others we should focus on our own growth and development.

If you have found love, great! Keep working on it consistently.

If you haven't found anyone then there are chances that you may find your partner when you least expect it. Love can happen anytime, anywhere. Maybe, you might fall in love with someone instantly. We all have heard about *"love at first sight"* or watched it in movies, but is it actually possible?

The idea is wonderfully romantic and yes, it can happen. You may immediately realize that person is *"the one"* in the very first time you see them. Within seconds (or even less), your brain knows if it is interested in who it is looking at. There is a chemical reaction in your brain. High levels of dopamine and a related hormone, norepinephrine, are released during attraction. These chemicals make us giddy, energetic and euphoric, even leading to decreased appetite and insomnia – which means you actually can be so *"in love"* that you don't feel like eating or sleeping!

Many experts also explain the love at first sight as a halo effect. The *"what is beautiful is good"* phenomenon is a type of halo effect, in which people who are judged as beautiful are also judged to have more socially desirable personality traits, to be more likely to succeed in their jobs and to be better partners. From this split-second judgment of attraction, we potentially infer qualities about the person that would make them a good partner and even someone we are likely to love. Love at first sight can happen multiple times, and many times it never translates into a relationship and is often forgotten.

You may have had experiences of getting instantly attracted to a stranger at random locations like shopping mall, theatre, library, train, flight, airport etc. but you know that you will never meet them again and you simply feel good about seeing them and then you move on. So, basically love at first sight is nothing but physical attraction and a gut feeling you have that a person can be a great potential partner. It may work and it may not. Don't worry if you didn't experience love at first sight with the person you are dating. What really matters is everything that happens in your relationship after that first meeting — and building shared experiences and memories with them that could end up lasting a lifetime.

In the end, I just want to say that romantic relationships are great but the best and most important relationship which you can have is with **yourself**. First, fall in love with yourself and be happy. Accept yourself with all your flaws because being imperfectly authentic is perfectly awesome. We all need to take out time for ourselves and to do things that give us a sense of happiness, purpose and fulfillment, irrespective of our relationship status. It is extremely important to be yourself. If you like to fall in love fast – fall in love fast and don't let anyone shame you by calling you clingy or needy. If you are distant, be distant and explore the wonderful world around you. It is impossible to find love if you are wearing a mask all the time. Always remember to prioritize your own emotional, mental and physical health.

If you are happy and content with yourself, then only you will be able to give happiness to your partner and be in a blissful relationship. Live life as per your terms as long as you are not harming others.

"Learn to adjust but never compromise."

Follow your heart and do what actually makes you happy. People, who make their life decisions based on social pressures or opinions of others, end up regretting a lot at a later stage and often go through a mid-life crisis. It is better to do what you like and face consequences of your own wrong choices instead of suffering because of other's advices. Choose your partner based on your criteria and who is good for you — not someone who is good for your parents or relatives. Not someone who is good for your bank balance or for your image but someone who makes your life fulfilling and loves you till their last breath.

Our previous generations were often told that they were subservient and not good enough as the rest of the world but the youth today, has access to everything like any other person in the world. You have the platform and the freedom to fly high and chase your dreams. Utilize this opportunity and aim for the best for yourself and people around you. Dare to dream big and have faith in yourself. Each and every one of you reading this is an important person. You don't need to be better than others. You simply need to be better than what you were yesterday. Be the best version of yourself and keep evolving and learning things constantly.

Be kind. Kindness is the most important element of satisfaction and stability in a relationship. Kindness makes each partner feel cared for, understood, validated and loved. A great deal of evidence shows that the more someone receives or witnesses kindness, the more they will be kind themselves, which leads to upward spirals of love and generosity in a relationship.

Just live your life to the fullest with your partner. The more experiences you share together as a couple both positive or negative, it will further deepen your bond. Your relationship is like a plant. You need to water it daily, make sure it gets proper sunlight, protect it by taking it inside your house in case of heavy rain and eventually one day it will grow into a beautiful tree and you will get to enjoy its shade, fruits and flowers.

There will also be times when you get your heart broken. But with love, your shattered hearts will heal again. It is love that fuels the journey of our soul but sometimes we will have to endure the pain in order to understand what actual happiness of being in love is.

A fascinating reality of love is that it is not time bound. It is not something which you should find before you turn 30 or by any other standard set by the society.

However, it is important to be "open" to positivity and welcome love from people and the universe. Don't stress about finding love.

It will somehow find you. If you are on the lookout, ready to share a part of your life with your partner and if you are willing to say yes to the challenges they hold, they will come more and more frequently.

"Great long lasting relationships don't just happen. They take time, patience, persistence, honesty and two people who truly want to be together."

AFTERWORD

"Witnessing a lot of close friends going through depression due to their relationship issues and frequently reading about young individuals becoming alcoholics, drug addicts and committing suicide because of their failure in love, has prompted and inspired me to write this book. A lot of social media surveys, sampling and personal interactions have been done for my research to get different perspectives on several important issues which shall feature in the book."

- Rudra Dave

This book is the perfect present to gift your friends or relatives who fall in the below categories :-

1. Singles waiting for their soul mate,

2. People who are about to get married,

3. Young couples who want to learn the secret of a successful and long lasting relationship,

4. Teenagers and adolescents who are exploring the world and discovering themselves,

5. People who are stuck in a toxic relationship or are going through a heart break or a separation.

ABOUT THE AUTHOR

Rudra Dave is a young Author, Life Coach, Motivational Speaker and a Chartered Accountant who attains a great sense of satisfaction in motivating others to achieve their goals, actively solving their problems and helping them to build a happier, meaningful and successful life.

His other interests include Reading World Literature, Watching Movies, Travelling, Martial Arts, Stock market, Debating, Food Blogging, Playing Sports (competed in Chess, Table Tennis and Skating at the State level), Discovering Spirituality (certified holder of second level degree in Reiki Natural Healing and Yoga) and enhancing his IQ (Intelligence Quotient), EQ (Emotional Quotient) and SQ (Spiritual Quotient) by trying to constantly learn, improve and evolve with each passing day.